norwegian touches

Flat bread plate and ale tankard, Skattebu Cottage (eighteenth century),
Valdres Folk Museum, Fagernes, Norway

Stave church
Nesbyen, Hallingdal, Norway

Norwegian Touches

History, Recipes, Folk Arts

Notably Norwegian Revised and Expanded

Bordbønnen
Grace Before the Meal
This beautiful painting by Herbjørn Gausta is in the fine art collection of
Vesterheim Norwegian-American Museum, Decorah, Iowa.

Compiled by Louise Roalson and Joan Liffring-Zug Bourret

Penfield
BOOKS

Kitchen window in a private residence, Hundorp, Norway

© Penfield Books 2003

ISBN 1-932043-17-9   Library of Congress Control Number: 2003106248

Contents

Recipes

Vesterheim photo

Vesterheim Norwegian-American Museum, Decorah, Iowa

Dedication: To Dr. Marion John Nelson, Vesterheim director 1964–1999, and his wife, Lila, first curator of textiles and registrar. Vesterheim is now the nation's finest folk art museum devoted to a single immigrant culture. In 1978, His Majesty Olav V, King of Norway, awarded Dr. Nelson the Knight's Cross, First Class, in the Royal Norwegian Order of St. Olaf for his service to Norwegian and Norwegian-American society and culture. The Sons of Norway awarded him its Leif Ericson Citation, and St. Olaf College, Northfield, Minnesota, bestowed upon him an honorary degree in 1992. Mrs. Nelson recieved the St. Olaf Medal in 2000 from the Norwegian government.

Front cover: *Arla Erickson Lyon of Decorah, Iowa, bakes* kransekake *professionally. The background shows a Vesterheim cupboard, a reproduction of one used in Gudbrandsdal in the late nineteenth century, that was generally placed near the door for pans of soured milk to be eaten as a pudding or to stir into water for a drink. The* åklæ *(coverlet) is one using a traditional Norwegian tapestry technique. This example has the eight-petal flower of the type made in Sogn and dates from the late eighteenth century. A recipe for* kransekake *(ring cake) is found on pages 132–133.*

Thank you to all whose recipes and essays are in this book and to many others, including the Vesterheim staff.

Photographs are by Joan Liffring-Zug Bourret unless otherwise credited.

Editors included: Maureen Patterson, Dorothy Crum, Melinda Bradnan, Miriam Canter, Julie Eisele, and Douglas "Dag" and Sharon Rossman.

Graphics: Molly Cook, M.A. Cook Design. Printed by Pella Printing

Books by Mail: This book postpaid $19.95
Penfield Books, 215 Brown Street, Iowa City, Iowa 52245

Marilyn Skaugstad of Iowa City, Iowa, baked the treats shown on the back cover. Her nostalgic essay about family baking and identification of the foods shown here are on page 158. Marilyn is wearing part of her grandmother's Hardanger costume with her own American blouse, typical of American Norwegians who, since the early 1900s, mixed treasured clothing worn by their Norwegian ancestors with their own styles. Many examples of attire from Norway with added American elements are in the Vesterheim collection. Authentic bunads are available from Norway.

Inside front and back covers:

The mountain ash rowan with its bright red berries was photographed beside a Norwegian home. Mythology specialist and Norwegian-American Douglas "Dag" Rossman of Decorah writes, "In the Norse myth about Thor's visit to the giant Geirrod's hall, it was a rowan tree growing beside the river Vimur that provided the Thunder God an opportunity to save himself and Loki from drowning. In the Celtic world, the tree was also thought to be a protection against witches and lightning. The berries were used for healing, and the branches for divination."

Dag honors his Norwegian heritage as a storyteller and author. His great-great-great grandfather was the last of his ancestors to be born, in 1805, on the Skattebu farm. The Skattebu cottage is preserved at the Valdres Folk Museum, Fagernes, Norway. The interior of the cottage is shown on page one.

Dates to Remember

12,000 B.C. People were living in the areas of Norway where the ice mass of the last glacier was receding. Hunting and fishing were the major sources of livelihood. A 4,000-year-old rock carving depicts a human figure on skis.

A.D. 800–1000 For pillaging, trading, or settling, Norwegian Vikings sailed to England, Scotland, Ireland, Normandy (France), the Isle of Man, the Hebrides, Spain, Sicily, and the Near East. In 874 Iceland was settled by Norwegians. The Icelandic Althing (parliament), established about 930, is the world's oldest legislative body. In 982 Eric the Red discovered Greenland and named this ice-covered land for the stretch of green he found along the southern coast, which the Norwegians settled.

1002–1030 Leif Ericson, thought by some to be the son of Eric the Red, landed on the east coast of North America, calling it "Vinland" because of grapevines he found growing there. House foundations and other artifacts discovered on Newfoundland in 1963 are believed to be from Norse settlers who were in America nearly five centuries before Columbus. In 1030 Norway was converted to Christianity by King Olaf Haraldsson, also known as St. Olaf. Special rights of inheritance that protected the oldest son in retention of land dated from this time, now changed in favor of the oldest child.

1066 William the Conqueror, seventh-generation Viking ruler of Normandy, conquered England, built Windsor Castle, and became the first Norman king of England.

Mid–1300s Black Plague killed almost half the population.

1387–1814 Norway was ruled by kings of Denmark. In **1814** the Treaty of Kiel penalized Denmark for its support of Napoleon by giving Norway to Sweden. Before the transition was carried out, Norway declared itself independent. The constitution, the parliament, and a degree of independence were retained even after Norway became subject to the Swedish crown.

1825 The first Norwegian ship, the *Restauration*, organized for emigration, sailed to the United States. The population of Norway at this time was about one million.

Above: *The cloister ruins of a Benedictine monastery founded in 1103 are on the island of Selje. Above these ruins are the ruins of St. Michael's church and St. Sunniva's cave, where legend says she was martyred for refusing to renounce her Christian faith. The island is on the west coast of Norway.*
Left: *View of the site of Borgundkaupangen, a Middle Ages (1030–1536) market town near Ålesund. Depressions in the earth indicate building sites. Some building sites are displayed in-situ nearby.*

1835–1924 At least 750,000 Norwegians emigrated to America. Still, the population more than doubled in Norway as a result of smallpox vaccination, better nutrition made possible by the introduction of the potato from America, and other health advances. Today there are over 3½ million Norwegian Americans. This is only slightly less than the present population of Norway.

1905 Norway declared its complete independence. Charles, brother of King Christian X of Denmark, became King Haakon VII of Norway.

1914 World War I began; Norway remained neutral, but many of its ships were sunk by submarines.

1917 Norwegian Lutheran Church in America was formed as a union of three synods—Norwegian and Hans Nielsen Hauge's, both dating from the 1840s, and the United Norwegian Lutheran Church, which was formed in 1890. The total membership was 1,200,000. In 1960 Lutheran Church in America (the word "Norwegian" had been dropped in 1946) merged into the new American Lutheran Church.

1940–45 Norway was occupied by Nazi Germany. There was active Norwegian resistance.

1946 Norway became a founding member of the United Nations; Trygve Lie of Norway, his country's foreign minister at that time, was elected U.N. Secretary General.

1957 King Haakon VII died and was succeeded by his son, King Olav V. King Olav's ancestry traces back thirty-four generations to King Harald the Fairhaired, who united Norway in 872.

1960 Oil drilling in the North Sea off the coast of Norway near the city of Stavanger brought prosperity to Norway.

1975 150th anniversary of the first modern emigration to America; His Majesty King Olav V came to America for the Sesquicentennial.

1991–1999 His Majesty Olav V, King of Norway, died. He was succeeded by his son, His Majesty Harald V. In 1995 their Majesties Harald V and Sonja, King and Queen of Norway, toured the United States and visited Vesterheim Museum.

Historic Buildings at Vesterheim

*The Valdres house, with three rooms built around 1800, came to
America through the efforts of the Iowa Bicentennial Commission,
private individuals, and the Valdres Folk Museum in Fagernes, Norway.
The privy belongs to the nearby Wickney house, a museum gift moved
from North Dakota, as was the Bethania Lutheran Church.*

Beauty and Style in Norway

A private home near Vågå has this wonderful scenery.

Right: *A view over the valley west of Vågå in Gudbrandsdal shows Jotunheimen Nasjonal Park.*

The building, above, once a small farmhouse, now carefully restored and furnished, is often rented as a honeymoon cottage. It is part of the farmstead shown below. The Farmers/Conservation Center for Traditional Rural Culture aids with preservation to maintain viable working farms.

Right: *Examples of traditional farm fencing at the Valdres Folk Museum, Fagernes, Norway.* Skigard *is the term used for slab-wood fencing, which uses the outer slabs of the tree—waste material from the sawmills— in a unique, functional "hog tight" fence found throughout rural Norway. The fence in the foreground, middle, is made of woven saplings (wattle), a similar technique often found in the wall construction of Viking-age buildings. These photographs show sites visited on the Vesterheim Architectural Tour in 2000 led by Darrell Henning, Vesterheim Curator.*

Ingestion of the fly agaric mushroom shown on the grounds of Valdres Folk Museum produces a feeling of increased strength and agility, followed by hallucinations and, finally, by a loss of awareness.
—Dag Rossman

Historic Norwegian Settlement

Otternes Bygdemuseum farming site was occupied continuously for centuries. Some of the twenty-six buildings date from the seventeenth century. The last occupant was in the 1980s. The site overlooks the picturesque Aurlands Fjord near Flåm.

Norway the Nation

Once primarily rural with each family self-reliant, Norway today is prosperous and industrialized. The majority of the 4.5 million people live in urban areas. Ninety-nine percent of adults are literate. Oil drilling in the North Sea has brought new prosperity to Norway. One of northern Europe's tallest buildings is in Oslo, the capital city.

Fifty years ago, about one-fourth of the working population of Norway was engaged in farming, forestry, and fishing. The oldest industry, fishing is still healthy. Norway ranks high in the world in quantity taken from the seas. Much of the catch is exported. Norway exports aluminum, ferro-alloys, nitrate fertilizers, tools, machinery, ships, oil, and electronics and telecommunications products.

Traditionally a seafaring nation, Norway has a merchant fleet carrying goods between different foreign ports. Norway's coastline is 15,000 miles long. Three-fourths of the people live within 10 miles of salt water. Norway is so mountainous that only 4 percent of its 125,000 square miles is cultivated. Cattle and sheep graze in the mountains.

Along the coasts are fifty thousand islands that help to protect the mainland from storms. Norway has about seventeen hundred glaciers. The waterfalls are spectacular and have been harnessed for hydro-electric energy. Narrow fjords reach as far as 100 miles inland from the sea. Some are only 500 yards across, yet the mountains on either side are up to 5,700 feet high. The longest is Sognefjord.

Almost one-fourth of the country is forest land, mostly spruce and pine, but also birch and other deciduous trees.

Winters are long. Norway is snow-covered for four to six months. The weather is fairly mild, however, because of the Gulf Stream, which flows north along the coast, keeping ports ice-free year round.

The period of the Midnight Sun—when the sun never sinks below the horizon—is longer the further north you go. In Tromsø, the largest city in North Norway, this period is May 20–July 23. Hammerfest is the northernmost town in the world.

In area, Norway is the fifth-largest European country, but in population density it is the lowest, except for Iceland. The only native minority group is the Sami, who live in the north. Ten percent of the Sami lead the traditional nomadic life of reindeer herders.

There are two official languages in Norway—standard Norwegian *(bokmål)* and New Norwegian *(nynorsk). Nynorsk* is based on local dialects.

Norway is a parliamentary democracy. The king is the head of state; executive power is in the cabinet under the prime minister.

Norway is noted for worldwide contributions from its creative artists and for its unique folk arts, developed province by province due to mountains and isolation from the rest of Europe. No longer isolated due to technology and communications, Norway participates in seeking peaceful solutions to world problems. The museum at Maihaugen shows the history of Norway from hunter-trappers to participation as leaders and neighbors in the greater world beyond the isolating mountains and fjords. A sign announces, "We are no longer alone."

Newspaper Links to Norway and America

Between 1865 and 1914 there were 565 newspapers and magazines in the United States printed in the Norwegian language. Today there are two with some text in Norwegian: *The Western Viking* of Seattle and *Norway Times* of Brooklyn.

Honoring Norwegian Heritage

A Norwegian-American immigrant family monument in bronze, "The Promise of America" statuary, sculpted by Clifford J. Carlson, of an 1860s Norwegian immigrant family with two children, is in Lake Mills, Iowa, on six acres of restored prairie. The statuary was dedicated in gratitude "to all immigrants who settled on the prairies so long ago . . ."

Leif Erickson statues are on both coasts, East and West, with sites named after the noted Viking who came to America first—before Columbus.

Communities with large populations of Norwegian Americans fly the flags of both countries.

The Royal Norwegian Embassy in Washington, D.C., has a strong role in supporting Norwegian-American culture throughout the United States. Their web site offers current news and events of interest.

An American Norwegian's Year in Norway

Excerpts by Andrea Cowles Nelson

There is a long history behind Norway's system of democratic socialism. Much of it stems from the fact that up until the twentieth century the majority of Norwegians were extremely poor, if not starving. . . . "Equality" is a most important concept to the majority of Norwegians, perhaps because for centuries they did live under such a strict class system. Tired of bowing and scraping to the upper classes (land owners, business owners, the state, and often the church), and tired of scratching an existence out of a country with less than 5 percent of the land arable, the modern Norwegian seems to feel it is worth the taxes necessary to eliminate poverty. There is also a sense that no one should make a display of wealth, and great pride in the fact that even the king often uses the mass transportation systems just like the average citizen. They place a premium on living with simplicity to the extent that if one does have a vacation cabin in the mountains, it shouldn't need a lot of "frills." Some even feel that indoor plumbing and electricity in vacation *hyttes* are extravagant. The newspapers carry extreme criticism of wealthier people like the famous skier, Bjørn Dahle, who are starting to build elegant chalets with many rooms and luxuries. It seems it is just not *norsk* to flaunt it.

Days are long and dark now. The last two weeks of December will have fewer than five hours of daylight, and that time between 10:00 and 3:00 is usually light gray rather than bright sunshine. Temperatures hover around freezing, so moisture often comes down as rain or sleet rather than snow, causing extremely icy conditions. Therefore, all cars have changed wheels for winter to *piggdekker* (studded tires), and even bicycles have donned *piggdekker* for winter. Because walking is so dangerous on the ice, and the salting and sanding that we are all so familiar with in the northern states of the U.S. are nearly nonexistent in the villages here, people of all ages use their *sparks* (kick-sleds). They act as a sort of "walker" on runners that one uses for balance with one foot on top of a runner and the other kicking the ground to propel the sled forward. They are fantastic for getting around town quickly and safely: for hauling groceries, school books, backpacks, or for hauling another person on the seat in front of the handlebars. *Sparks* come in all sizes and we see people from ages six through one hundred using them. It's rather embarrassing to be shuffling along on the ice trying to stay upright and to have a little gray-haired 80-year-old whoosh by on her *spark*. Because of the dark winter days the city of Hamar and the surrounding areas have miles and miles of lighted cross-country ski trails. The dark does not keep people inside, and the best prescription against depression (which is a definite problem here with the lack of sun) is to be outside skiing and *sparking* and biking under the lights. Homes have many lights left on all night long, and the Norwegians always light candles when guests arrive, which is a carry-over from the days when there was no electricity and candles were all made by hand and therefore very dear and used sparingly. But for a guest arriving in the dark, the candles were always lit. It is also truly warming to see rows and rows of electric candles in every window of every home when out on a dark day.

Sailing to America

Many Norwegian immigrants brought trunks with wooden utensils, clothing, and coverlets. A collection of mementos from the original voyage of the *Restauration* was given to Vesterheim Norwegian-American Museum, where they can be seen today.

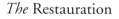

D.H.

The Restauration

Vesterheim photo

One family brought fine china.

20—

Norwegian Immigration

Norwegian Americans celebrate and remember the start of Norwegian emigration in 1825 to the New World. That was the year that the sloop *Restauration* sailed the Atlantic, bringing into New York harbor fifty-two Norwegians plus a baby born to the captain and his wife five weeks before the landing.

It was a long and perilous voyage (July 4 to October 9) undertaken by people who were aware of the dangers and who willingly risked their lives to reach the New World to become a part of its great challenge and to share its cherished freedoms. Described as "a small, one-masted vessel originally rigged fore-and-aft with a jib, mainsail, and often topsails and staysails," this "Norwegian *Mayflower*" was less than half the size of the 1620 *Mayflower.*

The man responsible for this adventure was Cleng Peerson, who spent three years in America and returned to Stavanger in 1824 to tell the people of religious freedom, political equality, and economic opportunity in America. Peerson met the group when the sloop arrived at New York.

The new Americans stayed together, settling in the Kendall area of New York state (near Buffalo) on the shore of Lake Ontario. There they spent the next ten years. It was from there that Peerson began a long walk first to Illinois and later to Texas in search of better sites.

The area Peerson selected was only 70 miles west and a little south of Chicago—the Fox River Valley with its rich, level and fertile land, today dotted with towns, two of which are named Norway and Stavanger. The migration from New York state to the Ottawa-La Salle county area of Illinois began in 1834. The fifty-three who arrived on the *Restauration*—so named because it was repaired and rebuilt for the voyage—became known as the "Sloopers." In 1925, the Slooper Society of America was organized to perpetuate the memory of the Sloopers.

Centennial Anniversary 1925

Address of President Coolidge before the Norwegian Centennial Celebration, at the Minnesota State Fair Grounds, June 8, 1925

. . . "In 1825, there arrived in New York a small sloop, the *Restauration*, with fifty-three Norwegian immigrants on board. This was the first large group of people from Norway who came to make their homes in the new land of the free across the Atlantic. This event marks the beginning of the steady stream of immigration from Norway, a country which has sent to our land a larger proportion of her population than any other country with the exception of Ireland. . . . The 'Sloopers' are by no means, however, the first Norwegians that are recorded in American history.

"They were the first deep-sea navigators. They pioneered the migrations which boldly struck across the western waters . . . But even before William of Normandy had conquered at Hastings, Leif the son of Erik, nearly five hundred years before Columbus, appears to have found the new world. . . . Among the fascinating chapters in the history of the dark ages is the story of Iceland. As a little Norse republic, it maintained itself for several centuries as one of the real repositories of ancient culture in a world whose lamp of learning seemed near to flickering out. We have long known of the noble Icelandic literature which was produced during those generations of the intellectual twilight . . .

"They found the western ocean, and it was a Norseman who first traversed the Bering strait and demonstrated that there was no land connection between Asia and North America . . .

". . . Within a very few years one of them first traversed the northwest passage from Atlantic to Pacific; and the same one, Amundsen, carried the flag of Norway to the south pole; and now, within a few days past, he has been the first to make large explorations in the region of the north pole in an airplane . . .

"The *Restauration* sailed from Stavanger, Norway, on July 4, 1825, with a desperately heavy cargo of iron and a party of fifty-two people. She came safely into the port of New York after a voyage of fourteen weeks, which compares with nine weeks required for the historic passage of the *Mayflower*.

". . . It was claimed that she was the smallest vessel that had ever made the trans-Atlantic crossing. The New York authorities threatened to deny her the privileges of the port on the ground that she carried too many passengers and too much cargo . . . Almost without money or supplies, the little company of immigrants was taken in charge by the New York Quakers who raised funds to send them to Kendall, Orleans County, New York. There they secured lands and established the first Norwegian settlement in this country . . . although the Norwegians are among the greatest seafaring peoples, this party was composed almost entirely of farmers, so that their first interest was to get land. And ever since, the greater share of Norwegians have come in search of homes on the land. Those first immigrants having practically no money bought a tract on the shore of Lake Ontario for $5 per acre to be paid for in ten annual installments . . .

"But it should be explained that while the settlement of 1825 in Orleans County, New York, was the first Norwegian settlement and represented the first organized immigration, these pioneers of the *Restauration* were not the first Norwegians to come here. Considerable numbers had come even before the Revolutionary War . . . There were Norwegians in both army and navy during the Revolution and the War of 1812. But the fact remains that the great movement which established Norwegian communities all over the northwest and contributed so greatly to the building of that part of the country began with the voyage of the *Restauration* . . . These Northmen, one of whose anniversaries we are celebrating today, have from their first appearance on the margin of history been the children of freedom. . . . Thousands of them volunteered in the service of the country during the Civil and Spanish wars, and tens of thousands in the World War. The institutions and the manners of democracy came naturally to them . . . You have given your pledge to the land of the free. The pledge of the Norwegian people has never yet gone unredeemed."

—*Excerpts from the* Decorah Posten,
published by the Anundsen Publishing Company
Decorah, Iowa

Artistic Norwegians

Human Realities Onstage: The Drama of Henrik Ibsen

The towering talent that was Norway's contribution to world drama could have languished in a provincial apothecary if Henrik Johan Ibsen had followed his youthful intention. Born at Skien on March 20, 1828, the shy, introspective lad moved to the coastal town of Grimstad to become a druggist's apprentice. Then he decided to study at the University in Oslo but was sidetracked by the theatrical scene in that city and Bergen.

Ibsen tried his hand at writing some imitative plays, but he soon recognized the dramatic possibilities of his own internal conflicts. The result was works of profound originality that caused shock, surprise, and enthusiasm—or condemnation—depending on one's view. He became the strongest creator of realistic, social, contemporary plays in the nineteenth century.

Ibsen's first masterpiece was *Brand,* written in 1866 and followed the next year by the beloved *Peer Gynt. A Doll's House* made him world famous, and he showed the perverted results of feminine frustration in modern society in *Hedda Gabler.*

Ibsen's final plays were judgments on his own life—unforgettable, poetic expressions of the questioning, disquieting time in which he lived and wrote. Every civilized person has been affected by his life and work—Norway's gift to the world.   —*Julie Jensen McDonald*

Storm and Rainbow: The Art of Edvard Munch

The paintings of Edvard Munch have much in common with the rugged, awesome scenery of his native Norway. They command attention and repay it with a deep thrill.

The artist who was born into a respectable, middle-class family in 1863, said, "We should stop painting interiors with people reading and women knitting. We should paint living people who breathe and feel and suffer and love." He did exactly that.

One of the best known works from Munch's monumental cycle of paintings, *The Frieze of Life,* is *The Scream,* and this is how he describes its genesis: "One evening I was walking along a path—on one side lay the city and below me the fjord. I was tired and ill. I stopped and looked out across the fjord—the sun was setting—the clouds were dyed red like blood. I felt a scream pass through nature; it seemed to me that I could hear the scream. I painted this picture—painted the clouds as real blood. The colors were screaming."

Munch's early exhibitions met with hostility, but his friend Henrik Ibsen told him, "The more the enemies, the more the friends."

The artist had gained considerable fame by the time of his death in 1944, and the universal significance of his work was fully appreciated by the 1960s. He is often referred to as the Father of Expressionism.

Munch was forced to sell some of his paintings in order to live, but in many cases he made a replica for himself. His prodigious body of work—one thousand paintings, forty-five hundred drawings and watercolors, and six sculptures—was willed to the city of Oslo. The Munch Museum at Tøyen, Oslo, was built between 1960 and 1963 to house this remarkable collection.   —*Julie Jensen McDonald*

Edvard Grieg

With composer Edvard Grieg (1843–1907) and others, there emerged a style of classical composition that often used Norwegian folk melodies and rhythms. Born of musical parents, Grieg was trained musically in the Germanic and Danish traditions. His awakening to the importance of Norwegian music came at age 21 when he spent a summer with the famed violin virtuoso Ole Bull, who was enthusiastic about the music of his native Norway. He also met Rikard Nordraak, a Norwegian nationalist composer who played and sang some of his own works.

Grieg's musical output from that time included the incidental music for Ibsen's *Peer Gynt,* the *Piano Concerto in A Minor,* many song cycles, character pieces for piano, and chamber music. Grieg achieved international recognition because his style was influenced by the folk melodies, harmonies, and rhythms of his native land, in contrast to the Germanic tradition on the continent. The Grieg Museum is in Bergen.

The Edvard Grieg Society, based in New York, fosters an appreciation of Grieg and of the rich cultural traditions of Scandinavia.

Music from Norway

Rikard Nordraak (1842 1866), who died tragically young, composed *"Ja, vi elsker dette landet"* ("Yes, We Love Our Native Land") with words by Bjørnstjerne Bjørnson. It was first performed in May, 1864, in celebration of the fiftieth anniversary of Norway's constitution.

Norwegian vocal music before the mid-nineteenth century existed in many forms, including the impressive cattle calls known as *lokke,* a combination of singing, shouting, and talking.

The performer, generally a woman, shouts words like *"koma da, barn, a stakkare"* ("come now, children, poor things"), calls the cows by name, sings wide vocal leaps, and vocalizes on a high pitch.

In traditional country vocal music a type of poetry was used that consisted of four lines of two nearly identical couplets called *stev.*

The Hardingfele violin (Hardanger fiddle) was played principally in western Norway from Hardanger to Sunnfjord and in the central valleys. It has a wealth of ornamental detail, short neck and fingerboard, and long "f" holes. Five sympathetic strings under the four that are played create a drone effect. Dances for which the Hardanger fiddle was played were in two overall rhythms. In triple time, the dances were called *springar, springleik, pols,* and *runnom.* In double time, they were called *halling, gangar,* and *ril.* Check the Hardanger Fiddle Association of America, which has thousands of members in North America.

In America, love of music motivates the popular male choruses and other musical groups for which the immigrant communities have been long noted. Simple folk songs from Norway have been sung by immigrant mothers as they rocked the cradle, and at house parties and community gatherings with accompaniment by fiddlers, accordionists, guitar players, and others.

The love of old-time Norwegian music has never died. Many communities also have musical festivals including folk dancing.

Judith Simundson of Dubuque, Iowa, who researches in Norway, has recorded and performed folklore and songs on CDs titled *Nordic Thunder: Tales & Songs of Winter Solstice* and *Norwegian Tales of Enchantment.* She performs extensively in schools and other locations.

Ole Bull and Sculptor Jacob Fjelde

In Europe, the Norwegian Ole Bull (1810–1880) is remembered as one of the great violinists of all time. He was conductor of an orchestra in Oslo and in 1832 he performed with Chopin.

In America, he is remembered for bringing eight hundred Norwegians in 1852 to Pennsylvania, where he had purchased 11,144 acres of land for a dollar an acre to provide homes for them. The sale proved to be fraudulent, and the settlers were forced to move on. Bull's first concert in the United States was in 1843. There is an Ole Bull State Park in Pennsylvania near "Oleana," as the land site was known. There is a monumental statue of Bull in Loring Park near downtown Minneapolis.

Hiawatha   *Ole Bull*

Sculptor Jacob Fjelde (1856–1896), born in Aalesund, Norway, came to Minneapolis in 1887. He is noted for sculptures of Ole Bull, above right, in Loring Park, of Hiawatha, above left, in Minnehaha Park, and of the miner figure in the public library, all in Minneapolis. His sisters were artists in embroidery work and tapestry weaving. His son, Paul, created the Lincoln Monument in Frogner Park in Oslo, Norway, and the statue of Col. Hans C. Heg, commander of the Fifteenth Wisconsin regiment during the Civil War in Lier, Norway. Replicas of the Heg sculpture are in Capitol Park, Madison, Wisconsin, and in Heg Park near Racine, Wisconsin.

—*From* My Minneapolis *by Carl G.O. Hansen, 1956*

Some to Remember

Sonja Henie, won the Olympic Games in figure skating and world championships from 1927–1936 and played in movies. She left Norway a major museum of modern art in Oslo.

Babe Didrikson, Olympic athlete
Sigrid Undset, Nobel Prize writer
Notre Dame coach Knute Rockne

Of Norwegian descent:
Arlene Dahl, Celeste Holm, Marilyn Monroe, Eliot Ness, Liv Ullmann, and many others

Business men: Conrad Hilton and Arthur Andersen

Politicians include two former vice presidents: Hubert Humphrey and Walter Mondale. Earl Warren served on the U.S. Supreme Court.

Others are listed with recipes or essays in this book. For more names and up-to-date information about Norway and Norwegian Americans, check the Internet. One site lists information about those who are half Norwegian on the mother's side!

Vesterheim collection

"And a Hardanger Fiddler Plays The Whole Cat" (Note that the fiddle is shaped and painted like a cat.) Carving by James Jacobson of Torrence, California (1932–1994)

28—

Giants and Names

There were giants in the earth in those days; and also after that, when the sons of God came in unto the daughters of men, and they bore children to them, the same became mighty men which were of old, men of renown.—Genesis VI:4

The ticket had come from his Uncle Jakob, who lived near Elk Point, South Dakota. At age twenty, Ole Edvart Rölvaag accepted the challenge and welcomed the opportunity. He left behind all that was familiar in his homeland in Lofoten in the district of Helgeland just below the Arctic Circle.

In America, he did farm work in South Dakota, studied at St. Olaf College, Northfield, Minnesota, and, back in his native land, at the University of Oslo.

From 1906 until his death in 1931, Rölvaag taught Norwegian literature at St. Olaf College. He also found time to create one of the masterpieces of American literature, *Giants in the Earth,* published in Norway in 1924, and then translated into English and published in America in 1927 by Harper & Brothers, now Harper & Row.

Giants in the Earth is must reading, not only for persons of Norwegian descent, but for all who would relive the many trials and triumphs of the hard wagon journey westward, the problems of the "great settling," and the heart-rending anxieties of decisions inescapable in accommodating to a land that was at once so strange and so full of hope.

Here we quote, not from the story, but from explanations of terms and names. In the preface of the 1964 Torchbook Edition of the Rölvaag novel, the late Einar Haugen, the distinguished scholar who was a professor of Scandinavian and Linguistics, Emeritus, at Harvard University, wrote:

"The word which is here translated as 'settling' or 'land-taking' is the Old Norse landnam, *a standard term for the settlement of Iceland by Norwegian Vikings in the ninth century. The proud chieftains who left Norway for the west a thousand years earlier form a romantic backdrop to the humble settlers of our own time."*

In a footnote about names, Rölvaag wrote: *"The practice of changing surnames has gone on extensively with the Norwegian-American. Among the common folk in Norway it is quite customary even yet for the son to take his surname from his father's first name; the son of Hans must be Hansen or Hanson. Likewise the girl; if she is the daughter of Hans, her surname becomes Hansdatter (Hans' daughter), which she retains even after marriage. When the Norwegians became independent landowners in America their slumbering sense of the historical fitness of things awoke, and so many of them adopted the name of the place they had come from in the old country. Hence the many American names now ending in –dahl, –fjeld, –gaard, –stad, etc. . . ."* (O.E. Rölvaag: *Giants in the Earth, 1964; Torchbook Edition, courtesy Harper & Row, Publishers, Inc., New York.)*

"The Letter"

They came in 1865 "because of the letter." It was from their son, Sven, in Decorah, Iowa. They would need him; none of them knew a word of English. But when Gunnel Svenson Korsgaard and his family arrived in Decorah, they learned that Sven had enlisted in the Union Army. He died at age nineteen in Andersonville, a prison camp.

"Gunnel" translated into English as Gunder, and the place they settled near Decorah became known as Gunder, Iowa. Great-great-grandfather was buried at the Lutheran Cemetery in Gunder as "Gunnel Svenson Korsgaard," the latter for their farm home in Norway. But except for Rachel Gunderson Korsgaard, the children all took the name Gunderson. The boys were Knute and Peter Gunderson. By marriage, three girls became Aanestad, Ellings, and Skarshaug. My great-grandmother Gunhilde chose not the Norwegian youth her father liked, but a Swiss immigrant named John Lang. She left by covered wagon on her honeymoon because of her family's displeasure about the marriage.

Gunhilde knew no German and John knew no Norwegian, so they learned English together. They bought land near Remsen in northwest Iowa and enjoyed a long and happy life. Gunhilde pieced a baby quilt for her son, named Samuel (anglicized) after Sven, her deceased brother.

This quilt was of the American style like those made by her neighbors, not solid Norwegian weaving. We gave this quilt to Vesterheim. Samuel married my grandmother, Eva Adora Penfield, daughter of a Civil War veteran and descendant of a Penfield military officer who came to New England in 1638 in the service of the king of England.

—*Joan Liffring-Zug Bourret, Publisher*

The Home, Barn, Church, and School Left Behind

Barn for sheep

The Gunderson family's one-room home built in the 1700s

Above: *School at Kongsberg*

Byron Gunderson stands by the traditional corner fireplace. The cupboard in the house, painted June 23, 1838, credits Peter Knudsen Korsgaurden.

Left: *The Bygdethun Stavkirke, built in 1711, Kongsberg*

Byron Gunderson, Glenwood, Minnesota, visited Korsgaarten, the ancestral home of his immigrant ancestors, and supplied these photos. He is the grand-nephew of the publisher's great-grandmother Gunhilde. Many of the descendants of Gunnel Svenson Korsgaard have visted this site in Hardangervidda. Gunnel's wife, Kari, died before the family came to America.

Home in America

Erik P. Egge, an early Norwegian settler in Winneshiek County, Iowa, built a log home for his family in the early 1850s. In the winter of 1853, the Egges shared the home with the newly arrived Reverend Ulrik Vilhelm Koren and his bride, Elisabeth. The home was moved to Luther College in 1913 and became the first element of Vesterheim Museum's Open Air Division.

Norsk Utvandrermuseum in Norway

This open-air museum and research center along the shores of Lake Mjøsa near downtown Hamar opened in 1989 and is devoted to the story of Norwegian emigration. Buildings from America on the grounds include the log house of Peder Borderud from Kindred, North Dakota; a granary from the Bjørgo farm in northeast Iowa; a one-room house from Vining, Minnesota, built by Knut Gunderson, and a corncrib from southwest Wisconsin. The Sacquitne barn from northeast Iowa was moved there. The museum also has a research center with letters, photographs, and archival information. The genealogical society offers assistance.

Vesterheim Genealogical Center & Naeseth Library

Vesterheim Genealogical Center & Naeseth Library has grown to become one of the leading genealogical research centers in the United States. Gerhard B. Naeseth was appointed director in 1974 and began the center's work out of his home in Madison, Wisconsin. The center was later housed at the University of Wisconsin Memorial Library in Madison. Eventually a suitable building was found and purchased in January of 1993 at 415 West Main Street, Madison.

Naeseth had a strong commitment to the study and preservation of history and genealogical information about the Norwegian immigrants who settled in the United States. His original research materials and book collections, as well as materials donated or purchased through generous donations, make up the present collection.

This collection includes: many rolls of microfilm of Norwegian church records and some U.S. church records; transcripts of cemetery, census, and church records; obituaries and the Rowberg collection of obituaries; Norwegian and U.S. local histories; family histories, and much more.

Vesterheim Genealogical Center staff are ready to help with Norwegian research projects. They have a great deal of experience in Norwegian genealogical research and willingly interpret records one may find while working on a project. Staff members and volunteers representing VGC & NL are at any number of outreach locations throughout the United States. Classes are held at least four times a year including sessions on writing family histories, and many advanced genealogical topics. The staff also leads a tour to the Family History Center Library in Salt Lake City, Utah, every two years.

Please call any weekday from 9 a.m. to 5 p.m. to make an appointment to visit Vesterheim Genealogical Center & Naeseth Library.

—Carol Culbertson, Director
Vesterheim Genealogical Center & Naeseth Library

Tracing Fourteen Generations

Belest and Martha Roalson, 1864

Their names, for fourteen generations we can trace, were: Belest Lauvsnes, Belest Belestson Lauvsnes, Belest Belestson, Roald Belestson, Belest Roaldson, Roald Belestson, Eli Roald, Byre Roald (who married Ola Olsson), Roald Olsson, Belest Roalson (who emigrated to America), Oscar Roalson, John Roalson, and our children, Eric, Brad, and Craig Roalson, and grandchildren Benjamin, Jeffrey, Jacob, and Daniel.

Actually the man who emigrated to America was Belest Byröe of the Island of Byre, near Fister, Norway. Belest's ancestors had lived on this island for at least ten generations. Belest Byröe married Martha Oledatter of Suldahl. Both were twenty-eight years old when they came to America, settling near Ossian, Iowa. In America, people had difficulty pronouncing Byröe, so Belest followed the Norwegian custom of adding "son" to his father's name. He became Belest Roaldson, but the "d" was soon dropped.

Belest died of cancer at age forty-two. Martha died in 1932 at age eighty-eight and was survived by seven children and thirty-one grandchildren, one of whom was my husband, John, who died in 1992.

—*Louise Roalson*

Note from Daryl Roalson, Duluth, Minnesota:
Roalson genealogy supplied by relatives still farming at Byre traces to the historic tenth-century kings and queens.

Photos courtesy Daryl Roalson

A widow at age 42, Martha Roalson is shown with her children in 1932. Left to right, rear: Sanna, Oscar, and Martha. Front, from left: Roal, Marie, Ole, Ellen, Mother Martha, and Belle. These children and thousands of others with Norwegian heritage lived contributory lives in America.

Pioneer Ministers and a Diary

His name was Elling Eielsen, and he became the first ordained Lutheran minister in America. A lay preacher, he came to America and settled near Racine, Wisconsin. From there he walked to New York to order the first catechism printed in English for his use in teaching the Norwegian settlers and the Indians. He was ordained in New York. He went to Illinois, ministering to the Sloopers who came on the ship the *Restauration* in 1825. Reverend Eielsen built an addition to his cabin in Wisconsin for his niece, Gertrude Severson, the great-grandmother of Clarice Roalson of Duluth.

Another renowned minister was Ulrik Vilhelm Koren, who brought his wife, Elisabeth, to America and to Decorah, Iowa. There, they and their son, Paul, served Norwegian immigrants and their descendants for seventy-two years, from 1853 to 1925.

The Diary of Elisabeth Koren, documenting pioneer life, continues in print, a classic in immigrant literature about the era.

A National Museum in Iowa

In 1825, the first vessel carrying Norwegian immigrants to America landed on the shores of this country. These early immigrants risked everything to follow their dream of a new life. They were determined to expand their horizons in an unknown, untamed land, relying on faith, family, and hard work. Their stories of survival and success contribute to the intricate fabric of American history.

Soon after Norwegian immigrants arrived in their *vesterheim,* their "western home," they started building a museum. It began in 1877 as a small general collection for the benefit of Luther College students. Twenty years later, the college made the visionary decision to focus on collecting Norwegian immigrant materials. The museum about pioneers itself became a pioneer in preserving cultural heritage, making Norwegians one of the first groups in America to do so.

For 125 years, Vesterheim has preserved rich stories and traditions in the heart of Norwegian America. In his nineteenth-century book about a Luther College seminary student, Peer Strømme writes, "Such is the picture that flashes upon the inward eye and warms the heart when one sees or hears the name Decorah. It has come to mean a great deal to those who spent the happiest days of their youth there, where their horizons were widened. . . . It has come to mean a great deal, too, to all people of Norwegian descent, for a focal point of their spiritual and cultural life." Knut Gjerset, the museum curator in the 1920s and 1930s, commented that the museum found "favorable soil" in the Norwegian-American community of Decorah.

Since its inception, Vesterheim has built the largest and most comprehensive ethnic museum in the country—an internationally renowned, world-class museum in the heart of Iowa. The museum has grown from a study collection to a museum of twenty-four thousand artifacts and sixteen historic buildings, visited by seventeen thousand people each year, and a genealogical center with an unparalleled collection of records telling the stories of individual Norwegian immigrants.

Yet Vesterheim is much more than a Decorah museum. Vesterheim is your museum, whether you are a rosemaler in Idaho, an anesthesiologist in Chicago, or a lefse lover in Arizona. The "western home" we have built now stretches across America. Our more than seven thousand members come from every state and several foreign countries. Celebrations of Norwegian-American heritage are in evidence from San Diego to Stoughton, Wisconsin, to New York City. Even though Norwegian-American artifacts find their home in Decorah, the stories they tell are value their cultural heritage.

People will continue to find meaning in the objects from their pasts. Acting as a good steward of such objects, and using them to help people make connections, is the most important thing we do at Vesterheim. As an ethnic museum, Vesterheim takes on the special task of not just displaying objects but representing people's identity, and nothing is more important than that.

In an age where maintaining a distinct cultural identity becomes more and more difficult, it becomes critical to know who you are and where you came from. This knowledge provides the compass, the touchstone, for everything else we do in life. That is why we work so hard to preserve Norwegian-American culture—sharing this cultural legacy can inspire people of all backgrounds to celebrate tradition.

—*Janet Blohm Pultz, Executive Director of Vesterheim*

Vesterheim Museum Hours

The museum is open daily May to October except holidays, and Tuesday to Sunday, November to April. Each year the museum offers special events, including Nordic Fest, the last full weekend in July, a citywide event featuring traditional music, arts and crafts, foods, and other activities. In addition, each year the museum hosts several week-long adventures in learning: Elderhostel programs, folk art classes and special exhibits to emphasize Norwegian-American history and culture.

The Western Home
Vesterheim Norwegian-American Museum
An Early Beginning

Vesterheim Museum traces its origin to 1877, when Luther College started a study collection for its students. The college started systematically collecting immigrant materials in 1895 when large numbers of Norwegian immigrants were still arriving in the United States every year. At the same time, many tools and trades that earlier immigrants had brought were becoming obsolete by the turn of the century. Therefore, the museum sought examples of household objects and farm tools that might have otherwise been thrown away.

Vesterheim's Open Air Division started in 1913 when the museum moved a historic building to Decorah, the Egge-Koren home that housed the first Norwegian Lutheran pastor west of the Mississippi River. Reverend Ulrik Vilhelm Koren and his wife, Elisabeth, arrived in Winneshiek County, Iowa, in 1853. The local community had not yet completed building the parsonage, so the Korens spent their first winter in the home of the Egge family. Ultimately, the Korens served the congregations around Decorah for over fifty years—and helped found Luther College—but their first home in America was the modest one-room house they shared with the Egges.

Elisabeth Koren kept a diary during that period that remains a vivid depiction of pioneer life. Her writing provides the descriptions of the house and what happened there that helped the museum recreate the 1853 interior. "The house is fourteen by sixteen feet, divided by curtains of calico into two rooms, one of which affords space for two beds, which extend along one wall of the house and are separated from each other by a second curtain. . . . Helene [Egge], who appears to be a kind, friendly woman, brought out beer and *fattigmansbakkels* for us; after that, accompanied by Per and Kari, three and four years old, we went up to the loft to put our things somewhat in order. I cannot imagine how Vilhelm will get any quiet for study here, it will be so crowded."

In 1925, Norwegian Americans marked the centennial with many lasting contributions to their legacy: the Luther College museum officially became the Norwegian-American Historical Museum (it would be re-named "Vesterheim" in the 1960s); the Norwegian-American Historical Association was founded in Northfield, Minnesota, through St. Olaf College; and the museums in Norway honored the Norwegians in America with a large gift of Norwegian artifacts.

The museum moved to a site in downtown Decorah in 1933, and ultimately became independent of Luther College in 1964. The museum complex grew to incorporate original downtown structures, historic buildings moved to the site, and more facilities in distant locations: the Vesterheim Genealogical Center and Naeseth Library is in Madison, Wisconsin; the Washington Prairie Methodist Church is several miles outside of Decorah; and the Jacobson Farmstead is also on its original site several miles outside of Decorah, restored to its 1913 condition.

Telling the Stories of Everyday Life

Lars Davidson Reque arrived in Deerfield, Wisconsin, around 1840. As he started to clear farmland, build his barn, house, and outbuildings, plant

Kubberulle, *a wagon with log wheels, built by Lars Davidson Reque*
Vesterheim photo

crops, and tend livestock, he did not have the ready cash available to purchase a professionally made wagon. Instead, Reque did what many immigrants did—he built his own wagon out of hand-hewn lumber with solid logs for wheels. Though roughly made, a *kubberulle* (log-wheeled wagon) could serve for years. The Reque *kubberulle* even served as a wedding carriage in 1844 when Lars Reque and his fiancée set out for the nearest Justice of the Peace, fourteen miles away. By the 1890s, when this *kubberulle* was acquired for the museum, it was one of the few examples remaining; by the twenty-first century, it is probably the only surviving example of this once-necessary transportation. The *kubberulle* and artifacts like it preserve the living and working environment of early Norwegian Americans, a part of history that might very easily have been lost.

—*Tova Brandt, Vesterheim Curator*

The Arts at Vesterheim

Over three thousand artworks reflecting immigrant lives and talents have been gathered at Vesterheim in a variety of styles, from romanticism to social realism. Norwegian landscape paintings kept Norwegian Americans in touch with the land and culture of their ancestors. The artists responded to their new environment with portraits of distinguished Americans, scenes of children and home life, and American landscape paintings.

They also depicted the diverse society which they encountered, from New York construction workers to Native Americans, from gamblers to grandmothers. Eighty-five Norwegian-American women artists are among the five hundred artists represented at Vesterheim. Their naturalistic landscapes, charming floral still-life compositions, and strong portraits show that these women deserve to be better known as American artists. Vesterheim holds a significant portion of altar paintings from Norwegian immigrant churches that are still inspiring to the visitor today.

—*Carol Hasvold, Vesterheim Registrar and Librarian*

Norwegian and Norwegian-American Textiles

More than sixty-five hundred objects, including textiles brought from Norway and textiles made or purchased in the United States by Americans of Norwegian descent, are in Vesterheim's textile and costume collection. The greater proportion includes textiles representing Norwegian-Americans' lives in their new western home.

The immigrants first brought clothing and woven wool coverlets, called *åklær,* to use on the ship, and textiles and textile tools for use in the New World. Many brought spinning wheels, looms, or at least some of parts of the looms . . . Finally, there were the objects that were too important to leave behind, like the *mangletre,* a mangle board that would have been carved as an engagement gift, or parts of folk costumes (including jewelry) that likely had already been handed down several generations.

Norwegian women easily went from sewing their clothing in Norway to sewing their clothing in America, a task lightened by the availability, especially after the Civil War, of ready-made clothing for men and boys. Women continued to knit for their families, often with wool raised on their own farms. They didn't have to weave fabric for clothing; they could buy inexpensive cloth here. The looms were used to weave household basics, like blankets and rugs. The handwoven coverlets that the immigrants had brought with them were not fashionable in America, so they were quickly replaced with quilts. Norway did not have a quilt-making tradition so the immigrants had to learn to make quilts.

Traditional textiles inspire artists today. Weavers, for example, find patterns in the old coverlets that can be adapted to table runners and wall hangings.

The origin of *Hardangersøm,* Norwegian counted thread embroidery with cut and drawn work, is shrouded in mystery. Norwegian Hardanger embroidery has existed since at least the mid-1700s. Some believe that it came from Italy or is an offshoot of Danish cutwork *hedebo.* A surprising fact, considering its worldwide appeal today, is that historically this embroidery was only done in the county of Hordaland on the west coast of Norway. There it was known as *hvitsøm,* white work, and is identified by its specific stitches and techniques. Traditionally it was worked in white linen thread on handwoven white linen fabric, and only for trim on blouses, aprons, and other garments. Hardanger embroidery became a popular Victorian needlework. German pattern book companies were the first to promote the technique. American thread manufacturers began to publish patterns for Norwegian drawn work, as it was then known, after representatives toured Norway around 1895.

All sorts of textiles were embellished with *Hardangersøm,* from table linens to clothing. American women of all backgrounds enjoyed Hardanger embroidery, but women of Norwegian descent took a special interest in it as a way to express their heritage and at the same time make themselves and their homes look stylish. Immigrant women expanded the tradition by adding color to their American *Hardangersøm.* They were excited by the new materials that were available and took advantage of the inexpensive embroidery yarns and cotton fabric. They added borders of crochet and bobbin lace. Hardanger embroidery is now more popular in the United States than in Norway. Vesterheim has more than three hundred textiles, both Norwegian and American-made, embellished with Hardanger embroidery.

Woven Coverlets

The traditional bed covering of rural Norway is the *åkle,* or woven coverlet. Women wove them in their farm homes from the wool of the native *spelsau* sheep. The average size of *åklær*, five by six feet, relates to the dimensions of Norway's corner beds and the width of the looms.

Åklær were important for both warmth and color. The earliest Norwegian farm homes had dark, windowless rooms with dirt floors and soot-covered walls from a central fire. One way to add color and a festive feeling on special occasions was to hang the woven coverlets around the room. These textiles continued to be valued as decorative objects long after fireplaces with chimneys were introduced and glass and paint were more widely used.

Norwegians incorporated *åklær* into their rites of passage: at baptisms, marriages, and funerals. In some cases, protective symbols, such as crosses, were woven in. Many *åklær* were passed down through families and used at special events for generations. New bedding was necessary because beds in America were larger than in Norway. The quickly constructed immigrant log homes were drafty, and even the heavy wool coverlets were inadequate for the cold winters of the Midwest. A wide variety of weaves was used for coverlets. Perhaps the most widely used technique was *krokbragd* or boundweave. This twill-weave structure creates layers of floating yarns on the back, which makes these coverlets especially warm. Small geometric patterns are characteristic of this weave. The designs on *rutevev* coverlets are built up of square blocks. These "square weave" coverlets were most common on the west coast of Norway, but were also woven in the south-central districts of Vest-Agder, Aust-Agder, and Hallingdal. The *åttebladsrose* or eight-petal flower is a very common motif. Stylized lilies, crosses, diamonds, and knots were other popular motifs.

The colorful designs on *skillbragd* coverlets float over the surface, which is why they are also known as "overshot" coverlets. Coverlets in this weave are found throughout Norway. *Telemarksvev* is a variation characterized by lozenge or lemon shapes. *Tavlebragd* or monk's belt is characterized by block shapes. In north Norway, these textiles were often sewn to sheepskin for added warmth. Because this is a time-consuming weave, overshot coverlets often had special uses. Coverlets were important objects during rites of passage. They were used at baptism as christening blankets, during weddings as kneelers, and at funerals as coffin covers.

The warm pile sides of *rye* coverlets were considered the back. The pile side was placed down over the sleeper in the bed and the flat weave side showed on top. Some scholars believe that the *rye* developed as a more durable version of sheep pelt blankets. Fishermen tried to use pelts as bedding on boats, but the salt water made the leather stiff. Woven wool *ryer* stayed flexible. They were also common throughout Norway in farm homes. The northernmost version of the coverlet is a striped *grene* used by Sami. They were usually natural white and natural black wool with occasional additions of red and blue. Solid stripes alternate with a small pattern, used also in other parts of Norway.

—*Laurann Gilbertson, Vesterheim Textile Curator*

Editor's Note: Examples of textiles may be found in color on page 71.

Folk Art Emphasis

Vesterheim Museum is one of the only places that offers folk-art students the opportunity to study from a collection of historic pieces while taking a class. From first offering rosemaling instruction in 1967, Vesterheim's folk art program has grown to dozens of classes each year in rosemaling, woodworking, weaving, knife-making, cooking, and other aspects of traditional Norwegian culture. Instructors from Norway and America share their skills in classes that range from three hours to five days.

Vesterheim was one of the first museums to introduce the "folk" museum concept in America, according to Dr. Marion John Nelson: "It differs from the usual museum in placing its emphasis on the common man and in concerning itself with total outdoor environments as well as individual objects."

Vesterheim Open Air Division

The heritage of Norwegian immigrants to America appears not only in folk arts, festivals, and cookbooks, but also in historic buildings. The Open Air Division at Vesterheim includes a variety of historic structures, many representing the everyday lives of Norwegian immigrants and Norwegian Americans. The collection of structures—both within the museum's downtown complex and at sites located outside of Decorah— preserve the historical context for much of the collection and the people whose lives the collection represents.

An early log home from northeastern Iowa contrasts with a later frame house from the North Dakota prairie to demonstrate the increasing affluence as Norwegian immigrant families settled into their land. A house moved from Valdres, Norway, and a non-Norwegian house from Decorah offer the opportunity to compare the domestic architecture and interiors of Norway, Norwegian Americans, and the "Yankee" culture of the United States. A blacksmith shop, grist mill, and storage buildings preserve workplace structures. A schoolhouse and a North Dakota church represent community gathering places for learning and worship. In addition, a complete farmstead and a Norwegian Methodist Church are part of the

Vesterheim collection, but have been maintained at their original sites near Decorah to preserve not only the historic structures but also the historic landscape. Here are some examples:

Painter-Bernatz Mill, built in 1851 and restored to 1900 appearance in 1970, houses Vesterheim's exhibits of early Norwegian-American industry. Agriculture, woodworking, and metalworking are all highlighted as integral parts of Norwegian-American livelihood.

Egge-Koren House, built in the early 1850s in Winneshiek County, Iowa. This one-room log home is typical of the first houses built by early immigrants. For several months in 1853–1854, the Egge family also sheltered Rev. Ulrik Vilhelm Koren and his wife, Elisabeth. Elisabeth Koren's published diary, available from Vesterheim, remains a vivid depiction of life in a Norwegian immigrant community.

The Valdres House, shown on page eleven, from Valdres, Norway, still has its original furniture and painted walls of the 1800s. The house offers a look into the homes that immigrants left behind when they came to America.

What was once a common sight on the prairies—the white, steepled church—is preserved in Vesterheim's Open Air Division. The Bethania Church was built in 1903 in Northwood, North Dakota, and moved to Vesterheim in 1992. Both the church building itself and all of the interior furnishings remain intact, although hundreds of miles away from the original site.

Jacobson Farmstead, established in 1850 and restored to its appearance in 1913, is preserved in its original location and is a rare example of a farm complex in which the many specialized outbuildings survive. Still surrounded by active agriculture, the Jacobson Farmstead preserves an important period in rural history.

Washington Prairie Methodist Church, built from 1863 to 1868, was an early home to a congregation of Norwegian-born Methodists. This structure is still on its original site several miles outside Decorah. Its founder was Ole Peterson, a Norwegian immigrant who had been converted to Methodism after arriving in the United States. Peterson later returned to Norway to found the first Methodist church there.

—*Tova Brandt, Vesterheim Curator*

Where the Norwegians Settled

Life on the East Coast

There were Norwegians and Danes among the Dutch who founded New Amsterdam, which became New York City in the 1600s, and in those days, Norway was under the Danish king. Norwegian seamen served in both the Danish navy and merchant marine, and there were many Norwegian seamen sailing for the Dutch.

The Ellis Island Museum has the American Immigrant Wall of Honor, which includes Norwegian names. Emigrant information may be found on-line with ancestral names and arrival dates. The Sloopers in 1825 were the first of many waves of Norwegians settling across America. For many Norwegians coming to the United States, New York City was the port of entry. For some, the journey had been long enough and they were ready to call New York home. The Bay Ridge section of Brooklyn became the heart of the New York Norwegian community and celebrates May 17, Norwegian Constitution Day. Festivities are in Leif Erikson Park in Bay Ridge. Special performers include members of the Norwegian Folkdance Society.

Since 1997, a month-long celebration features *Norwegian Christmas at Union Station,* highlighting traditional and contemporary culture at various sites throughout Washington, D.C. A Christmas tree is sponsored by Oslo.

Syttende Mai, Norwegian Constitution Day, May 17, is celebrated in many American cities by organizations sponsoring parades and festivities.

Midwest Heritage

Thousands of Norwegians homesteaded lands in Minnesota, Wisconsin, Illinois, Iowa and the Dakotas. At an annual Høstfest in Minot, North Dakota, someone lamented the windy, rainy cold weather to a newsman from Norway. Thinking of the hillside mountain farming in Norway, he quickly responded that the "weather doesn't matter when you look at this beautiful land." There is a mention in folklore of the Dakota farmer who built a hill in memory of the mountains of Norway.

Illinois Heritage

I know the Norwegians from Illinois. Most of them have done well, and no immigrants have served America better than they have.

—Abraham Lincoln

Quoted in Nordisk Tidende, *7 Jun 1923. (A.N. Rygg "Norwegians in New York," published 1941, p. 48) From research by Jerry Rosholt. The majority of Norwegian immigrants in the Civil War and the best known Norwegian regiments were in Wisconsin units.*

The Sloopers, who arrived in the United States in 1825, eventually settled the Fox River Valley in Illinois in 1834. It was five years before they were joined by a lay minister. He was Elling Eielsen, who was born in Voss, Norway. The church building that is now the Norsk Museum was built in 1849 by his congregation. The museum is dedicated "to the memory of the Rev. Elling Eielsen, first Norwegian Lutheran pastor in America." The village of Norway is on the Cleng Peerson Memorial Highway (No. 71). It is the site of the Norsk Museum, the Cleng Peerson Memorial Park, the J. Hart Rosdail Memorial, and the National Norwegian-American Memorial. Peerson also led Norwegian immigrants to Texas.

From an ancient burial mound in Norway, the *Gokstad* ship, which sailed the seas in the eighth and ninth centuries, was unearthed in 1880. Magnus Andersen saw in this discovery an opportunity to prove that Vikings could have discovered America. He raised funds, built an exact replica of the *Gokstadskip,* and in a twenty-eight-day voyage with twelve oarsmen he sailed from Bergen right up to Chicago's lakefront for the 1893 World's Columbian Exposition. Restoration efforts have come from Scandinavian organizations. Another replica of this ship, built by the Leif Ericson Viking Ship, Inc., sails on Chesapeake Bay.

Sons of Norway

The Sons of Norway is the largest and most enduring of the Norwegian-American organizations. Founded in Minneapolis in 1896 and modeled after American fraternal lodges, it started as a mutual aid fund and later became a large insurance company with cultural programs.

Woodworking, Stabburs, and Stave Churches

Many styles of Norwegian woodcarving that evolved over the three centuries are displayed in the Vesterheim galleries. Dragon-style carving features elaborately intertwined figures. Carving appears in this style on artifacts from Viking burial sites, on early stave churches, and later in the nineteenth century when the dragon style inspired a revival.

Acanthus carving arrived in Norway in the eighteenth century from Baroque Europe. The richly textured acanthus leaves flourish on church altars and cupboards alike. The acanthus motif became popular in painted decoration as well. Chip carving, predating acanthus carving, uses V-shaped grooves to create a geometric pattern across the wood surface.

Chip carving is known in many other parts of the world. Figure carving in Norway can trace its roots to the animal forms found on horse-handled ale bowls, mangle boards, or other household goods. Burnt decoration and *kolrosing* are other Norwegian methods of decorating the surface of wooden objects. Patterns can be applied using heated irons with decorative shapes, or by incising a pattern and applying a darkening powder.

—Tova Brandt, Vesterheim Curator

Epcot in Florida
The Norwegian pavilion has a replica of a *stavkirke* at Walt Disney World® in Orlando.

Skogfjorden
The Norwegian language camp, sponsored by Concordia College, Moorhead, Minnesota, is one of the International Language Villages. It is on Turtle River Lake, north of Bemidji, where campers and visitors learn traditions and customs as well as the mother language.

Stavkirke *at Skogfjorden*

Little Norway: Valley of the Elves

A replica of a twelfth-century stavkirke, *a Norwegian timbered church from the Chicago Exposition of 1893, is now at Little Norway, above, in a beautiful timbered valley 25 miles west of Madison near Blue Mounds, Wisconsin. Dragon heads at the peaks of the gables were carved in Trondheim. Open to the public May to October, this building and many other pioneer structures tell of early life for Norwegian farmers in Wisconsin. Guides in costume lead the tours.*

Woodcarvers

Phillip Odden and his wife, Else Bigton, of Barronett, Wisconsin, are major woodcarvers in America. Phillip met Else at a woodworking school in Norway. They were married in 1978. Else is in her bunad *from Sunnmøre. Phillip's attire shows his Gudbrandsdalen heritage. Their lifestyle is Norway in America. Phillip and Else receive major commissions, and they teach students at their farm-workshop studio several times a year. Books and calendars feature their work and they raise fjord horses.*
See page 77.

Dragon-style drinking horn carved by Lars Kinsarvik (1846–1925) Displayed at the 1893 Columbian Exposition with other materials representing Norway, it was donated to Vesterheim in 2001 by Dr. and Mrs. Eugene J. Nordby in honor of Darrell Henning, curator, at his retirement.

Photo by Cliff Fredrick

The Gol Stave Church Museum in the Scandinavian Heritage Park in Minot, North Dakota, is a full-size replica of the stave church in Bygdøy Park in Oslo. That church was built in 1250 in Gol, Hollingdal, and, in the early 1800s, was moved to Bygdøy. The Minot stave church was a dream of Dr. Myron and Gail Peterson. Woodcarvers included their son, Steven, and Phillip Odden and Else Bigton.

The Chapel in the Hills
Rapid City, South Dakota

Left: An imported two-story stabbur *with a sod roof from Norway is the reception center for the chapel.* Stabburs *were used for storage of foods and supplies.*

Photos courtesy © Rushmore Photo & Gift

This building is a replica of a twelfth-century stave church in Borgund, Norway. The Rapid City chapel was built as a home for the Lutheran Vespers Radio Program by Arndt E. Dahl, banker, as a memorial to his parents, Pastor and Mrs. Anton A. Dahl. The chapel has columns with mask-like capitals, a stone altar, arches, and low backless benches. Erik Fridstrom of Norway carved the dragon heads on the roofs and highly decorated portals. Helge Christiansen carved the altar and the interior details.

Norse Mythology Carving for a Home

Phillip Odden carved the mantel for the Wisconsin lakeside home of David and Joan Floren of Wayzata, Minnesota. At left are panels from the portal of one of their buildings. Odden carves motifs from Norse mythology.

Thirst for Adventure

Moorhead, Minnesota's Heritage-Hjemkomst Center

A twentieth-century Viking ship and other exhibits tell the story of the Red River Valley, the trials and dreams of the early settlers, and the important heritage of today's children and adults.

The *Hjemkomst* (homecoming) Viking Ship, a vision of the late Robert Asp, was built of lumber from one hundred great white oaks. It sailed more than 6,100 miles in 1980 from Duluth, Minnesota, to Norway, and triggered the building of the beautiful center that is attracting visitors from many states. "Dare to Dream" is the theme. The theme fits the building of the Viking ship and the center, and passes on its challenge to visitors.

The Kensington Runestone

True believers think the stone with runic writing came from Viking sailors and explorers from Vinland in the year 1362. The stone has been buried in controversy ever since the 200-pound slab first surfaced in a field near Kensington in the early 1900s. Today it is in The Runestone Museum next to a statue of Big Ole in Alexandria, Minnesota.

The Kon-Tiki Raft

Norwegian Thor Heyerdahl and five companions sailed on the balsa-wood raft Kon-Tiki from Peru to the Tuanota Islands in eastern Polynesia, seeking to demonstrate that the islands could have been settled by Indians from America. *Kon-Tiki,* his book about the voyage, was published in 1950. Later, he wrote two other books: *Aku-Aku,* about Easter Island, and *Fatu-Hiva,* or "Back to Nature." A museum displays the raft and other memorabilia in Oslo, Norway. The museum is funding excavations in Peru to further explore if the Peruvian Indians were among the great seafaring peoples. Twelfth-century paintings on temple walls in Tacume show seagoing reed boats. Heyerdahl is but one of the Norwegians who sailed to explore the unknown. Another is Roald Amundsen, who reached the South Pole and adventured in the Arctic.

Norwegian Settlers

Lone Star Texans

The Institute of Texan Cultures in San Antonio highlights Norwegians and many others who came to Texas. The Norwegian Society of Texas keeps everyone in touch today. The first Norwegian settler was Johan Nordboe, self-taught painter and physician, who moved from the Fox River, Illinois, settlement of the Sloopers to a farm in Dallas County, Texas, between 1837 and 1841.

Henderson County, Texas, was the site of the first Norwegian settlement, called Normandy and later Brownsboro. It was founded by Johan Reinert Reiersen and his family. Like Norway, the landscape had high ridges and pine woods. A second settlement, called Four Mile Prairie, was founded by Reiersen on the border of Kaufman and Van Zandt counties in 1848 when the Texas government offered 640 acres free to families, 320 acres free to single men.

In 1849 Cleng Peerson, who founded the Illinois Fox River settlement, visited John Nordboe. When the Texas legislature created Bosque County in 1854, Cleng Peerson urged Norwegians to move into the area for better soil, water, and wood supplies. The Bosque Memorial Museum and an annual smorgasbord celebrate Norwegian heritage.

Other descendants of Norwegians in Texas are wheat farmers in Hansford County of the northern Texas panhandle.

West Coast Norwegian Heritage

Founded in 1979, the Nordic Heritage Museum of Seattle has a collection that tells the story of Scandinavian immigrants in the Pacific Northwest and the merging of their traditions and customs with American culture. Artifacts on display include skis donated by the Norwegian Ski Museum in Oslo. The museum has hosted exhibits and programs featuring weaving, rosemaling, wood carving, folk music, dance, and lectures. The nearby town of Poulsbo is noted for celebrating Norwegian heritage. Once, over 2,200 pounds of lutefisk were served at one of the annual dinners.

Norwegian-American Institutions

Nineteenth-century Lutheran Norwegian immigrants in America needed pastors. Founding colleges was one way to educate all the young qualified to attend because they did not know who would be called to serve. Courses in Norwegian are offered today by some of these colleges. State universities in Minnesota, Wisconsin, and Washington have strong programs in Scandinavian studies. Colleges with Norwegian roots include Luther College, Decorah, Iowa, and Augustana College, Sioux Falls, South Dakota. Minnesota has the most of any state with the following institutions: Augsburg College, Minneapolis; St. Olaf College, Northfield; Concordia College, Moorhead; Lutheran Theological Seminary, St. Paul; and Bethany College, Mankato.

St. Olaf and Luther colleges are internationally known for their famous choirs. St. Olaf is the site of the Norwegian-American Historical Association. Concordia College reaches thousands of young people through its International Language Villages, which include programs for adults.

Bethany College was originally founded by German Lutherans and later became sponsored by the conservative Reorganized Norwegian Synod. The East Coast has Wagner College on Staten Island in New York City. Two are on the West Coast with Pacific Lutheran University in Tacoma, Washington, and California Lutheran College in Thousand Oaks on land given by a Norwegian immigrant. Many have annual celebrations of their Norwegian heritage, particularly smorgasbords during the holiday season.

In a twentieth-century survey of Norwegian landmarks in America, many listings include buildings on these college campuses. For instance, Augustana College has the Berdahl-Rølvaag home. St. Olaf has the Rølvaag Library. There are hundreds of buildings, sites, and sculptures in the United States and a few in Canada of note. Leif Erickson is honored coast to coast.

Two historic churches still have a Sunday service in Norwegian: at Minnekirken in Chicago and Mindekirken in Minneapolis. There are also churches on either coast and in the gulf states for Norwegian seamen. Based at the Port of New York/New Jersey, the Seamen's Church Institute provides impressive services to meet the needs of the world's merchant mariners and the maritime industry. Its Centers for Seafarers' Rights, Maritime Education, and Seafarers' Services provide free counseling, referrals, advanced training, direct care, and ministry to merchant seamen worldwide.

Mount Horeb, Wisconsin
Fearless Troll Capital, USA

Trolls were feared for hundreds of years in Norway. These evil creatures were found in mountains, streams, and underground. In contrast, the *nisser* were charming little folk who hung around the barn and were fed porridge and milk, primarily at Christmas time.

Eric Werenskiold and Theodor Kittelsen were the first artists to illustrate the troll stories in Norwegian folklore.

No longer feared as evil, big trolls created in heavy plastic now migrate annually to the New World, where they stand guard as pleasant, amusing creatures. Trolls shaped by chainsaw artists and others decorate Mt. Horeb, which for several decades has proudly billed itself the troll capital of America.

The Troll Who Wonders About His Age
by Theodor Kittelsen

Growing up Norwegian American

by Rolf Frickson

At the age of three I was astonished to learn that I was smack dab in the middle of a community of mostly Bohemians and Poles with a few Danes and Germans thrown in. My parents had purchased a general store in Spruce, a tiny village six miles north of Oconto Falls and six miles west of Lena in northeastern Wisconsin. So it was from the first I learned that we and our neighbors were all different from each other. Bohemian and Polish were sometimes heard in the store where I stood and listened. My baby sister I called "Echtner" while other best friends had surnames like Christensen, Dudas, Hanek, Luisier, Nemecek, Rabas, and Treptow. It was less a melting pot than cultural diversity. Anyway, we were Norwegian and the only Norwegians there. (The Christensens were Danes.)

I surmised long afterward that my parents had grown up in nearly homogeneous Norwegian populations but thought of themselves more as Americans than anything else. Dad was pretty vague about how he fit into Norwegian immigration history, and I only learned much later he was fifth generation. Mom was more conscious of being Norwegian; her father had come from Norway as a boy, but she could speak only a few words such as "*takk for maten*" and say the prayer which begins, "*I Jesu navn*" . . . That, and count to ten.

In Spruce we became quite famous as a Norwegian family. Mother was a good cook and an especially good baker. She had known a few things from home, but her mother hadn't cooked many Norwegian dishes since she and her mother before her had been born in America.

In Spruce Mom found herself in stiff competition with good Bohemian and Polish cooks who brought tasty pastries to potlucks and parties. Who doesn't remember Bohemian *kolaches* or something called "kneecaps?" Mom felt she had to produce something just as good and thus set out to learn Norwegian recipes. Soon she was bringing golden brown trays of *krumkake, fattigmann, rosettes,* and *sandbakkels.* Her neighbors hadn't ever seen anything quite like these cookies and Mom was able to hold her own. From the Danes where we went to church up north in Maple Valley, Mom learned to bake kringle. She was not afraid to experiment, and hers always had the most filling, frosting, and crushed walnuts (her own touch). In Spruce her kringle were a big hit, too. I know I am not being partial by saying that they really were the best. Shortly before my fifth birthday (on November 18, 1945), Mama announced I was to have a birthday party and what did I want her to serve? To her astonishment my answer was, "I don't care as long as everything is Norwegian."

From there I suppose it was inevitable. Relatives gave me books about Norway. I recall one in which a girl and boy have an adventure in a *sæter*. Mama read it to my sister and me and recalled she had been told that our family, the Hovies, had had a *sæter* in Norway. The book somehow came more alive with that comment, and I reread the novel several times, although today I can't recall its name. There were other isolated incidents that were compelling, such as a Christmas letter in 1951 from *Tante* Berit of Milwaukee that announced that the last of the aunts, *Tante* Eveline Ramseth, had died in Norway. A letter in 1953 from Mom's Uncle Ivar in Northfield, Minnesota, asked for genealogical information for a cousin in Norway who was compiling a family tree.

No one in my family had ever visited Norway as far as I knew. No one seemed to want to, but I decided quite early on that I was going to go there. By the time I was to enter St. Olaf College, I had decided to take Norwegian (over the objections of my parents). In the first semester, Professor Esther Gulbrandsen assigned each of us to write term papers on our ancestry, and the next year, when Dr. Lloyd Hustvedt needed a student assistant from the Norwegian class to work for him in the archives of the Norwegian-American Historical Association, I took the job. Interests developed in these first two years at college have continued to sustain me.

I suppose that it wasn't that we as a family had maintained our Norwegianness, but more that we developed it in appreciation for what we met in others.

Editor's Note: The late Rolf H. Erickson, former board member of Vesterheim, was head of the circulation services department at Northwestern University in Evanston, Illinois. Co-editor for two books: From Fjord to Prairie *(Chicago 1976) and* Our Norwegian Immigrants *(Oslo, 1978), he also authored several articles on Norwegian-American history.*

Nourishing Inspiration

The little village of Saude, Iowa, which once had a country store, a blacksmith shop, a cooperative creamery, and a Lutheran church, took its name from the place in Telemark, Norway, where the ancestors of its most famous resident once lived. Only the church still stands, the church where Norman Ernest Borlaug, recipient of the 1970 Nobel Peace Prize, was baptized and confirmed.

Outside old Saude, near what is now Protivin, Iowa, is the farmstead of Borlaug's grandparents, where Norman was born in 1914 and lived with his parents for his first seven years. In 1921 his parents purchased an adjoining farm, where Borlaug spent the rest of his boyhood years, until leaving for the University of Minnesota at St. Paul.

The Norman Borlaug Heritage Foundation now owns the latter farmstead and has moved to the site the wooden schoolhouse where Borlaug received his elementary education. The foundation is a nonprofit corporation dedicated to promoting educational programs and projects that reflect the lifetime achievements and philosophy of Dr. Norman Borlaug.

Vesterheim has served for over fourteen years as a consulting agency to develop a long-range preservation plan for both sites and to assist in supervising the actual restoration. Steven Johnson, Vesterheim's deputy director, serves as the current Chair of the Norman Borlaug Heritage Foundation. The preservation of these farmsteads is especially fitting because, when the Nobel Prize was awarded to the self-effacing wizard of plant genetics, it was the first time such recognition had ever been given to a worker in the field of agriculture. And because Borlaug himself has been quoted as saying, "If it were not for the faith into which I was baptized and confirmed, and the ethics I grew up with in my home and my church, I would not be involved in this work today." That work has centered on a single humanistic goal: the eradication of hunger and abject poverty throughout the world.

Borlaug left his Iowa home to attend the University of Minnesota, but had to interrupt his forestry studies to make enough money to continue. It proved a fortuitous interruption because, as he worked with the urban poor in the Civilian Conservation Corps, his life values and future work began to take shape.

Norman Ernest Borlaug

The Mexican Ministry of Agriculture and the Rockefeller Foundation established a program to expand food production and, in 1944, Borlaug went to work for what is now known as the International Maize and Wheat Improvement Center. There he attempted to methodically select and breed wheat seed that could thrive where the soil was dry and depleted, insects and crop diseases were rampant, and farming was almost always by hand.

It was a project he and his team worked on for almost twenty years, but the results were well worth the struggle. Where once Mexico had to import 10 million bushels of wheat a year (more than half her supply), Mexican farmers now were able to harvest up to 105 bushels of Borlaug's "miracle wheat" per acre and, within four years, produced enough wheat to feed the nation's expanded population and have a surplus to export.

Because the wheat was highly adaptable to tropical and subtropical countries, India and Pakistan soon expressed interest and now have achieved or are nearing self-sufficiency. Over the intervening years, Borlaug has trained countless scientists from all over the world, who have helped expand his research to other crops, climates, and soils, earning him the title "Feeder of the World."

—*Charlie Langton, Vesterheim Editor*

Christmas Traditions in Norway

by Dr. Marion John Nelson

Long before the introduction of Christianity, a festival was held in Norway during the midwinter season. From it, Norwegian Christmas, that is to say, *Jul,* got its name. Much of Norwegian Christmas tradition is also carried over from pagan times. Two associations lingered especially: One is with fertility, the other is with the return of the dead.

Straw dominated in Christmas decorations until about one hundred years ago. Since pagan times it had been strewn on the floor through the major holidays. All the members of the household slept together on it, leaving the beds to the returning spirits of the dead. When the holidays were over, the straw was formed into animals, crosses, or men, which were thought to have protective power or to increase fertility. In some areas it was strewn on the fields to carry the fertility of the past growing season into the next. Massive mobiles called *uro* (unrest) were also made from the Christmas straw and hung above the table. The mystic powers of the universe were associated with it. All the above traditions continued into the 1800s.

The seeds that were the product of the straw were also important at Christmas. The first sheaf of grain cut in the fall was kept and tied to a pole put out on Christmas Eve. Originally this may have been an offering, but it was later associated with feeding the birds. If grain was found on the floor when the Christmas straw was removed, this was a sign of a good harvest for the coming year. Grain was also the material from which much of the Christmas food was made. In some places a large cake, perhaps the forerunner of *julekake,* was made for the Christmas season and eaten or distributed to guests with great ceremony. In other places individual cakes were made for members of the household, and the last crumbs from them were scattered on the fields to return fertility to the earth.

Porridge was the other form in which grain was eaten at Christmas. For this occasion it was made with sour cream rather than the usual milk or water. The resulting *rommegrøt* is still a standard Christmas Eve dish among Norwegians in America. Pork was probably the earliest meat associated with the Christmas season because the roasting of a pig had been part of the pagan festival. It is still a standard meat for Christmas Day, or in some areas, for Christmas Eve. The notorious lutefisk (dried cod soaked in lye water) was perhaps introduced as a Christmas Eve dish when this was a day of abstinence from meat in Catholic times. A fish pudding made in a fish-shaped mold for Christmas Eve may have had the same origin.

Just as the beds were left for the returning dead, so the table was left decked for their feasting. The ghosts who entered the house were generally ancestors who were friendly toward it, but if they were not properly provided for, they could take their revenge. The well-known *julenisse* (Christmas elf) was probably once such an ancestor, and he is to this day given his dish of porridge in the barns of Norwegian farms. His name derives from Saint Nicholas, but his character is of local origin.

Not all returning spirits were friendly. Those who had died an unnatural death swept through the air in great hordes and could bring destruction to the farm or carry off man and beast. One of these roaming spirits, called *Lussi,* was primarily concerned with seeing that all the ritual of the season had been properly carried out. These emissaries of darkness kept a note of fear in this otherwise joyous celebration of the coming light. To ward off evil, goat heads were carried on poles throughout the district by young people wearing furry robes. They would also make noise and demand refreshments on the farms they visited. The custom of children going *julebukk* between Christmas and New Year's, a practice not unlike our tricks or treats, continues the old tradition.

To symbolize that all the work except the essential was at a standstill during Christmas proper, the interior of the house was given a new character by painting geometric patterns in white lime or red earth along the top soot-covered logs of the wall or by hanging tapestries, coverlets, or ceremonial towels around the room.

New traditions, which either combined with or replaced those mentioned above, entered the Norwegian celebration of Christmas in the 1800s; major among these were the Christmas tree and the giving of presents. Evergreen branches largely replaced straw in the decorations. Candlelight on the trees was of major importance and remains so to this day. The custom probably developed from that of having a large candle in a pan of water burning continuously through the Christmas season.

Homemade decorations of paper also adorned the tree. Others took the form of baskets in which nuts, fruit, or candy would be placed. The tree was decorated by parents and kept hidden from the children until after the Christmas Eve meal. The door to the Christmas tree room was then opened and the distribution of presents occurred. In recent times these are sometimes brought by a member of the family dressed as the *julenisse*.

Because of the importance of boats to the Norwegians, a Christmas tree was even given a place on them. It was tied to the top of the mast on the fishing vessels waiting in harbor and was used as a symbol of the season on the mast of the great ocean liners that, until a few years ago, made their special Christmas trip from America to Norway with immigrants returning for the season.

The period covered by the celebration of Christmas in Norway varied at different times and in different places, but it was always long. The major preparations were to have been made by Saint Thomas Day on December 21, and recognition of the season should last at least though the day of the Holy Three Kings on January 6. Christmas could be chased out with brooms and noise-making on Saint Knut's Day, January 7. It was often allowed to remain until January 13, the day originally associated with midwinter.

Though many of the customs associated with Christmas in Norway did not originate for the celebrating of Christ's birth, the Christian message became associated with them. Sleeping on the straw became symbolic of Christ's manger bed and the equality of men. Candlelight, originally associated with the return of the sun, became symbolic of Christ's light. The Christmas Gospel was read before the meal on Christmas Eve, and songs conveying the Christian message were sung while marching around the Christmas tree before the presents were distributed. Christmas Day was spent in the church and in quiet contemplation of the season's meaning in the home.

Editor's Note: Dr. Marion John Nelson originally wrote this essay about Norwegian Christmas traditions for visitors to Vesterheim Norwegian-American Museum.

Advent Begins the Christmas Season in Norway

by Andrea Cowles Nelson

On a damp, bitter-cold evening, the first night of Advent, we hike downtown to watch the annual tree-lighting ceremony. To begin the ceremony, a parade of around fifty school-age children carrying burning torches comes trudging down a wide stairway from the street up above the town square. They circle the towering dark tree with their torches, and when they are in place, the crowd gathers behind them for singing carols. The mayor gives a short speech, and suddenly the tree comes alive with hundreds of sparkling white lights. The children are warned to watch for the *nisse* in the shadows under the tree and in all the nooks and crannies on their way home. (The *nisser* are the tiny little bearded men who run around helping everyone prepare for the holidays. Some are very helpful. Some play tricks to interfere with the Christmas baking and preparations.)

The ceremony ends with songs that have all sorts of motions to them, and the delightful part is to watch not only the children doing the poking, clapping, hopping, stomping, and bowing but also all of the adults prancing around to songs that obviously every person knows and has performed from childhood on. Everyone—toddlers, teenagers, parents, and grandparents—seemed to be enjoying the antics and the singing without the embarrassment that I suspect we might see and feel in a similar setting in the Midwest.

So holiday preparations are now in full swing, although I think Norwegians in the United States out-Norwegian those here with carrying on the traditions of baking the *sandbakelser, krumkake, rosettes, fattigmann,* kringle, and *julekake.* . . .

One of the traditions that has not disappeared is eating lutefisk—that "piece of cod that passes all understanding," dried and then preserved by soaking it in lye. We were invited to our first meal of lutefisk here last Friday night. The traditional meal is to serve the fish with a hot bacon dressing and mustard. It is delicious like that. Side dishes (in addition to *øl* and aquavit) are the usual boiled parsley-potatoes, (no butter) lefse, and *ertestuing*, a mashed-pea dish which they rave about, but which I could manage to live nicely without. When we told them that at lutefisk suppers in the U.S. it is traditional to serve meatballs and gravy, they looked shocked. Wide-eyed, they said, "On the same plate? At the same time?" They'd never heard of serving meatballs with fish. Here all my life I thought that was a custom straight from Norway. My husband suspects the meatballs were added to save the lives of the people who can hardly stand to look at lutefisk quivering on the platter. Perhaps the problem is that the immigrants who carry on the lutefisk tradition here in the United States have forgotten two vital accoutrements: the *øl* and aquavit.

Jul is the biggest holiday of the year in Norway, and advertising and preparations began already in October. Much is similar to the U.S. with gift buying, special foods, music, and decorating. But they do not decorate the homes until the very last week before Christmas, and many do not decorate the tree until Christmas Eve. Lights on the trees are all white, and trees are decorated simply with straw and hand-made ornaments. White lights gleam in all windows and on some trees outside, though the outdoor extravaganzas of colored lights common in the States are nonexistent and considered somewhat garish.

Special foods this time of year are *pinnekjøtt*, (a salted or smoked rack of lamb), lutefisk, *julepølse* (Christmas sausage), *medisterkaker* (spiced finely ground meat balls), and the many wonderful pastries such as *krumkake, fattigmann, sandbakelser, rosettes,* lefse, and *kransekake*. Although fish or lamb are the entrées in some of the western coastal areas on Christmas Eve, here in Eastern Norway, the meal is always *ribbe* (broasted beef ribs), *julepølser,* and *medistakaker,* sweet-sour red cabbage, potatoes, and pastries and rice-cream pudding with one almond hidden in it. No matter how full the children are, they keep eating the pudding until someone gets the almond, which "earns" them an extra small gift.

Rice-cream pudding is also placed in the barn for the *nisser,* the small creatures who help with and at times interfere with all the Christmas preparations. Families who no longer have a barn place the pudding in the garage or shed, and it always disappears.

One thing that the Norwegians make time for before Christmas is to either attend or perform in concerts. Just in the Hamar area there have been over one hundred concerts in the past month. I would guess one out of every four persons either sings in a chorus or plays an instrument in a band, and every musical group presents a concert before Christmas. These groups are interesting to watch as they contain such a mixture of ages. Many are community groups rather than school-sponsored, and so people from high school age through age one hundred can be in the same group. Concerts are often held in churches and some churches offer three or four concerts a week. We have gone to church on Sunday mornings to find twenty people or fewer at a service in a huge church, but find churches jam-packed for concerts. The children's choirs are delightful to hear as they sing out so clearly, and the adults seem to love to perform when in a group, which is interesting to see considering the inhibitions that one usually associates with the Norwegian personality. As one old gentleman said, "Without all the concerts, we could not get into the Christmas spirit."

Although people here seem every bit as busy with their holiday preparations as we do in the States, once Christmas arrives they stop everything. Hotels in Hamar are closed the entire time between Christmas and New Year's. Many businesses and all stores are closed for two to three days after Christmas, including all grocery stores. We were warned to stock up on food ahead of time. The celebrating continues on through the entire week up to and through New Year's Day with parties amongst family and friends. It is definitely a time for family to *slappe av*, to kick back, be lazy, and enjoy.

Fresh red tulips at Christmas time: That was what surprised me most in the homes we visited during the holidays. It was intriguing to stand in the flower shop on a Saturday afternoon and just watch the wonderful bouquets and combinations of plants being purchased, mostly by men. It is a time when friends and relatives are invited for parties, and one wouldn't think of going without bringing flowers. One of the more popular combinations was a red poinsettia, a purple African violet, and a bright yellow sort of flower all planted in the same basket—not colors we tend to think of for Christmas. Now between Christmas and New Year's, the flower shops still have huge bouquets of red tulips shipped across the North Sea from neighboring Holland in order to adorn the New Year's tables of appreciative hosts and hostesses.

Away in a Manger

In the Minnesota village of my childhood on the banks of two rivers flowing north, there were two little white churches. One was Presbyterian and one was Lutheran. My grandparents, with whom I lived in the country, took me to visit the Presbyterian Sunday School. Nearly all of the other children were "town" children. As a country child, I was frightened by their sophistication.

Our neighbor a quarter-mile away, Helma Lindquist, who was on our party-line phone, asked my grandmother if I could visit her Lutheran Church. It was there that I found immediately a very warm lap. Seeking love and warmth and security, I was charmed by the minister's pretty wife. One at a time, we were all held by Mrs. Gunderson, our Sunday School teacher. The other children were from the country, too. Because I was also of Norwegian descent, somehow I felt more comfortable with the Johnsons, Nelsons, and Sathers. Equally important was the opportunity to be in the Christmas program. Scandinavians love to sing. That is why I became a Lutheran at age five instead of a Presbyterian. Sometimes we went to church by boat when the rivers flooded the low spots in the road. Otherwise, we walked in from the country or rode in a wagon behind a team of horses or in the used cars of the 1930s. As Christmas neared, Grandfather hitched our brown riding horse with the Indian name Wawatasee, wearing Norwegian sleigh bells, to a little sleigh and Grandmother heated stones in the cookstove to warm our feet as we rode the two miles to the village for the Christmas program. Woods of poplar and pine stood out in the moonlight reflected on the crisp snow.

At the services, my friend Chummy and I held hands as we sang the cherished words of "Away in a manger, no crib for a bed, the little Lord Jesus lay down His sweet head." For our performance we received applause, hugs from Mrs. Gunderson, and hard red-and-white Christmas candies, special treats in the Great Depression. And there I found the love and the meaning of Christmas among our Scandinavian neighbors. No Christmas program has ever seemed so special and as lovely as this one more than seventy years ago in a village of the northland.

—*Joan Liffring-Zug Bourret, Penfield Publisher*

Decorative Arts and Crafts

This Christmas tree with straw decorations is outside the Selland-Forde immigrant log house at Vesterheim. The decorations are by Maryanne Esgate of Decorah, Iowa, who demonstrates the craft regularly at the museum. Straw ornaments were traditional Norwegian decorations. In the background is a 1910 name or membership quilt. Embroidered in various blocks are the names of twenty pioneer members of the Highland Lutheran Church near Decorah.

The Oneota Weavers Guild of Decorah made these decorations using techniques traditional to Norway. The skirt was crocheted in a traditional block pattern by Mary Nentwick of Long Prairie, Minnesota, mother of Lila Nelson of the Vesterheim Museum. Hanging in the background is an åklæ (coverlet) of wool and linen from western Norway, a type woven by farm women throughout the country. Åklær were used also as decorative hangings on other special occasions. The eight-petal flower motif is one of the oldest and most beloved of patterns.

Vesterheim Treasures

Coverlet, Åkle Hardanger, Norway
Early to mid-19th century wool on linen
Donor: Bergen Museum, Luther College Collection

Cotton doily
Minnie Magnuson Souris, North Dakota
Made as a 1936 Christmas gift for Floyd
Fairweather, donor

Quilt, Asborg Torsteinsdtr. Austenå Ramse,
cotton, circa 1850, Bosque County, Texas
Ramse made the quilt shortly after immigrating
from Tovdal, Aust-Agder, Norway.
Donor: Grace Rikansrud

Pictorial tapestry, Billedvev Gudbrandsdal,
Norway, mid-17th century, wool on linen
Tapestry was owned by Norwegian violinist Ole Bull
and his American second wife, Sara Thorp Bull.
Donor: Sylvea Bull Curtis

*Accomplished needleworker and teacher Grace Rikansrud of Decorah is wearing
the festive costume of Åmli, Aust-Agder, her ancestral home in southern
Norway. The Vesterheim ornaments were created by friends of the museum. The
items under the tree are worked in* klostersøm *and* Hardangersøm *by Grace.
The carved table was given as a bequest by Mrs. Jorgine Slettede Boomer, who
had it in her Waldorf-Astoria Hotel apartment in New York.*

Christmas in immigrant homes in America is recreated in the Selland-Forde log house at Vesterheim. The tree is decorated with homemade heart-shaped paper baskets traditional in Norway. Some of these came from a Norwegian-American farmstead near Decorah, Iowa, and date from the turn of the century. Others are made by Birgitte Christianson of Decorah. The baskets held candy for the children.

The home of the Selland and Forde families was built from one large pine tree in 1852–53 in Big Canoe Township, ten miles north of Decorah. Legend has it that seventeen people occupied this house during one winter in its early history. The birch bookshelf, dating from the late 1800s, was made by John Johnson Forthun for the pioneer home of Thomas O. Forthun south of Viroqua, Wisconsin. The shelf is of hand-planed boards and nailed construction, and has strong, primitive chip-carved decorations. The cradle is a typical immigrant cradle.

The rosemaling tree at Vesterheim is decorated in miniature wood cut-outs of objects that were part of Norwegian life: kubbestoler, *animals, mittens, Christmas trees, and others. Much of the contemporary rosemaling in the museum represents work by award winners in the annual national rosemaling exhibitions in Decorah. Surrounding the rosemaling tree, right, is work by award winners in the Vesterheim collection. The cupboard in the background was made by a Norwegian immigrant and painted by Martin Engseth of Minneapolis. It was part of a set of home furnishings belonging to Eleanor Hain of Minneapolis.*

Rosemaling

Rosemaling (decorative painting) is probably the best known Norwegian folk art. Its bold colors, graceful scrolls, and floral designs combine traditional styles that evolved over two centuries. Vesterheim's museum collection preserves the full history and development of this art form. Norwegians began rosemaling on household objects in the late eighteenth and early nineteenth centuries. In this early period, objects were decorated to emphasize a special purpose: trunks were decorated because they contained a girl's dowry; ale bowls were decorated because they were used on festive occasions; cupboards were decorated because they stored a family's valuables. Every valley in Norway developed its own style of rosemaling. Some styles are symmetrical, such as Hallingdal, while others are asymmetrical, such as Telemark. In the Valdres style, the rosemaling highlights bouquets of varied flowers, whereas the Telemark style uses intertwined scrolls and leaves. Both Vest-Agder and Os developed styles that feature stylized, symmetrical flowers.

When Norwegians immigrated to America, the trunks they carried often had rosemaling, as did some of the heirlooms they chose to bring with them. However, immigrants did not continue painting after they settled in the United States. Not until Per Lysne immigrated to Stoughton, Wisconsin, in 1907 did a Norwegian-trained rosemaler continue painting in the United States.

Many Norwegian-American families had old painted trunks or other family heirlooms that showed what rosemaling looked like, but Per Lysne was the first person to actively paint new pieces. Many of his neighbors and people who saw his work were inspired to try rosemaling for themselves, thus starting the rosemaling revival in America. Through the twentieth century, rosemalers studied examples of early Norwegian pieces and rediscovered the wide variety of styles with the rosemaling tradition.

Vesterheim Museum became a catalyst in the rosemaling revival when it began to offer rosemaling classes in 1967, especially by bringing instructors from Norway such as Sigmund Aarseth and Nils Ellingsgard. To this day, artists from Norway and America teach many classes each year in a variety of styles. The annual National Exhibition of Rosemaling continues to attract entries from all across the United States, demonstrating every year that this traditional art has a bright future.

—*Tova Brandt, Vesterheim Curator*

This cupboard is by the noted Ethel Kvalheim of Stoughton, Wisconsin.

Vesterheim photo

The Fjord Horse
Norwegian Style in Wisconsin

Ole Odden, age one, riding a fjord rocking horse carved by his father.

Woodcarvers Else Bigton and Phillip Odden and their son, Tor Ole, have an idyllic life on 80 acres in northwest Wisconsin. There they have, in addition to their barn studio lofts, a herd of fjord horses. These stocky, shorter horses have a thousand-year history of service in Norway. They come in five colors: yellow-dun, brown-dun, gray-dun, red-dun, and white-dun. Phillip competes in horse shows.

Loren Paulson photographed Phillip Odden in his hand-carved Viking sleigh with Ole bringing home the Christmas tree. Loren and his father, Robert, are noted photographers who have produced the Paulstad calendars with scenes of Norway, Sweden, and Finland for two decades.

Vesterheim photo

Bethania Church Altar

Bethania Lutheran Church was built in 1903 in Northwood, North Dakota, and moved to Vesterheim in 1992.

Vesterheim has a significant collection of church altar paintings by artists such as Herbjørn Gausta, August Klagstad, and Ole Balling. Altar paintings were important vehicles for communicating the Christian gospel to the members of the Norwegian immigrant churches and are still inspiring today.

Lars Christenson of Benson, Minnesota, an immigrant, carved this 12-1/2-foot-high by 10-foot-wide altarpiece in 1897–1904. Christenson adapted realistic illustrations from an American-printed Norwegian Bible of the 1890s to his own primitive style. Discouraged by lack of interest from the congregation for whom the work was intended, Christenson never completed it. Like a true primitive, he spread the figures over the surface of the panels with sound decorative or symbolic principles but with little regard for spatial relationships. After being exhibited at the 1904 Minnesota State Fair, the piece was stored until the death of the artist in 1910. It is displayed at Vesterheim Norwegian-American Museum in Decorah, Iowa.

A Norwegian-Style Dinner

*This table setting shows a dinner of Norwegian foods created by Marilyn
Skaugstad and Dwayne Bourret, Americans of Norwegian descent, who
combined their skills to cook the dishes shown above. After marinating it in
brown sugar and water overnight, Dwayne baked the six-pound salmon
with a combination of lingonberries and cranberries on top for
approximately one and a half hours at 375 degrees. The salmon is garnished
with dill, tomato wedges, and lemon slices.*

The Skaugstads' kubbestol *carved by Phillip Odden is at left. The rosemaled
plates, gnomes, elves, and costumed figures are all part of Marilyn's
collection of Norwegian folk art. Else Bigton's beautiful carved candle holder
in the center of the table sits on a Hardanger cloth. From left are salmon-
smoked rolls with cream cheese and an herb filling of dill, basil and parsley,
salt, and pepper. Steamed cauliflower is surrounded with small fresh peas
and Jarlsberg cheese sauce. There's also rum pudding with raspberry sauce,
rosettes,* lefse, krumkake, *and* kringla. *New potatoes are accented with
parsley. Cucumbers are marinated with white wine vinegar.*

norwegian foods

by Louise Roalson

Fish, fish, and more fish. Reindeer meat. Boiled potatoes served with every dinner. Herring, cheese, and sliced tomatoes for breakfast. Coffee breaks with lavish spreads of layered cakes and crisp cookies. A swallow of the native aquavit that burns all the way down.

These are among my culinary memories of a visit to Norway. On a three-day bus tour between Oslo and Bergen, the rousing strains of a Grieg concerto burst from the sound system of the bus. Daily fresh flowers were on the console between Knute, the driver, and Bjorn, the tour director. Craggy mountains, quiet lakes, clear mountain streams, tumultuous waterfalls, ungainly goats, red-cheeked children, and eleventh-century stave churches—all these are beautiful and not at all like America.

Why would my husband's grandparents leave such a beautiful country for the mid-American plains? Certainly not for the scenery. But leave it they did in 1872 with their six-month-old baby, Roal. Belest and Martha, both twenty-eight, packed their belongings, took a sailboat to Quebec, a train to Milwaukee, and an ox-drawn covered wagon to Iowa. They settled near Ossian in Winneshiek County in northeast Iowa. In 1876 they moved to the north-central Iowa area of Thor, in Humboldt County, where they bought a farm and built a sod house.

Belest and Martha banded together with other Norwegians to forge ties and friendships with those of like backgrounds. They shared the good times and the bad. Knowing little English, they clung to Norwegian ways, but the New World meant adapting to new foods.

Pork was one food that took some getting used to. In Norway it had been only a Christmas treat. Here, every farmer seemed to have plenty of pigs to slaughter. Bacon was something they had not been accustomed to eating.

Grøt was a favorite food. This hearty porridge made by boiling milk with flour was the main dish for many a pioneer meal. Its Norwegian origin goes back to ancient times. If rich cream is used instead of milk, it becomes *rømmegrøt*, which is considered a treat in Norwegian homes today.

Meat was not plentiful. Stews, soups, and meatballs were used to stretch what meat was available. These were (and are) delicious.

When there was lamb, there was *får i kål* (lamb and cabbage). This simple stew is popular in Norway. They missed the salt-water fish of their homeland—the cod, salmon, herring, and mackerel. Dried foods were not as common in America either, so they seldom fixed lutefisk, which calls for dried cod. Fish from Iowa streams were boiled and served with melted butter. Or they ended up in *fiskesuppe* (fish soup), *fiskeboller* (fish balls), or *fiskepudding* (a baked mixture of flaked fish and cream sauce). Today *fiskeboller* can be bought canned and *fiskepudding* remains popular in Norway, where it is served in some households once a week. There were boiled potatoes with meals, and dumplings were common. Potatoes were a base for lefse, a bread that is rolled thin and baked on a grill. As in Norway, the immigrants favored root vegetables that keep well over the winter. They grew carrots, cabbage, beets, onions, turnips, and rutabagas.

They didn't bother much with salads. Pickled beets or pickled cucumbers were considered salad enough, and still are in some Norwegian homes.

Fruits appeared on the table in the form of fruit soup, or sweet soup. This dish is far from ordinary soup. It is a mixture of fresh or dried fruits cooked with a thickening of tapioca. Into it goes whatever fruits are available—apples, plums, berries, cherries, peaches, and currants, for example. For the lingonberries *(tyttebær)* of Norway, these newcomers substituted the berries of America. Of course, they baked bread, using wheat and rye flour. In addition to the unleavened flatbread *(flatbrød)* they were used to, they now made yeast breads, too. For dessert there was *rødgrøt,* red fruit pudding made from red fruit juices, a sort of junket, plus various cakes and cookies. *Tilslørte bondepiker* (veiled peasant girls) was layered, buttered, and toasted bread crumbs, thickened fruit, and whipped "real" cream.

Special occasions called for special recipes—and still do. *Eggedosis* to celebrate Norway's Constitution Day, May 17, is easy to make, needing only beaten eggs and sugar. *Kransekake,* the national cake of Norway, was created to celebrate weddings, christenings, anniversaries, and birthdays. These concentric rings of almond-flavored cakes are sometimes stacked to a height of two feet. Today, among the new generations of Norwegians, there is an upsurge of interest in the Norwegian heritage, much of it involving food traditions. Making and serving dishes like those described in this book is a delicious way of participating.

Our Daily Bread

by Henrietta Oleson Bear

In the early 1900s, I spent most of my school vacations with my grandparents in Winneconne, Wisconsin. In this scrupulous Norwegian household there were two sets of dishes. One was of heavy ironstone, plain white, so heavy I could hardly lift the plates. These were for everyday use. The other set was daintier with an all-over pattern of brown leaves and azalea-like flowers. These dishes were kept in the yellow pine corner cupboard in the best sitting room and were used only when we had company. This was quite often because so many of our relatives and friends came regularly from the village of Winchester to shop. They brought baskets of eggs and cream from their farms and sat down to Grandma's noon dinners.

There were no telephones, but Grandma was always ready for these unannounced visits. There never seemed to be any flurry. The dinner, considerably embellished from the plain fare when we were alone, was on the table in no time, and all heads were bowed while Grandpa said grace in Norwegian.

In hindsight, perhaps I do know why Grandma was up to this situation. First, she knew her visitors and their shopping routines. After the noon meal they had to complete their shopping and get back home in time for chores. Second, the menu varied but little. We either had fried pork and milk gravy with boiled potatoes and carrots, or fried fish and fried potatoes with pickled beets. These menus were bolstered by homemade bread with butter and jelly. For dessert we had some of the white cake Grandpa baked every Saturday. And coffee, of course.

The big dining-sitting room was heated by an iron cookstove. On all but the hottest days of summer, it was used to cook the food, boil the coffee, and heat the water. In hot weather coffee was brewed fresh on the kerosene stove in the summer kitchen. Coffee was one of life's staples and no one came through our door without being offered a cup together with a large sour cream cookie that I and my playmates enjoyed immensely.

Grandma thought it was her duty to teach me to bake. I learned almost nothing, because I wanted so desperately to be out playing instead. In most of the homes on Water Street there was a hired girl to do the baking. Also, since my heart wasn't in it, my attention span was short and

Grandma's patience was even shorter; she would take the spoon from my hand and stir the batter herself. She would try me next on sifting flour, but there, too, I failed. The flour spilled over into the cupboard, which she told me was a sinful waste. I learned to scoop up every trace of it and pour it back into the bowl. In any event, there was no escaping until the baking was done. The ritual never varied. We made a white cake first, with jelly between the layers and a soggy meringue frosting on top. Then came the unfrosted, everyday molasses cake, and last the sour cream cookies. It all took until near noon, and by the time Grandma untied one of her long, gray aprons from around my neck, my friends, tired of waiting, were scattered all up and down the block.

We did the baking in the large pantry just off the dining-sitting room. All the cooking utensils were in cupboards there, as well as a pump with a galvanized sink and drain. There was a small table beside which, every afternoon at four o'clock, Grandma sat down for a cup of coffee and a sour cream cookie. If any of my friends were on hand and Grandma wasn't too busy, she made "coffee" for us, too—tiny little jelly sandwiches that fit on the precious three-inch butter pats that were part of her good china—a delight unsurpassed in our young lives. Now, more than fifty years later, two of those doll-sized saucers hang on a cypress wall in my Florida kitchen along with a collection of a hundred others inspired by the types I have treasured from my childhood.

Facing the street at the back of our lot was a small building that served now as a garage for Grandpa's car, one of the first Model T Fords in Winneconne. Returning from a trial run with this machine, Grandpa became confused between brake and gas lever and the car plunged straight through the end of the garage, boards cracking in every direction. Grandma, who had been looking out the window, flew out the door with me close behind to witness a rare upbraiding directed at her husband. Acquisition of this car was one of the few things they had seriously disagreed about, and Grandma was full of righteous indignation. She eventually rode in this machine, but mostly her journeys were spent in prayer. Grandpa's accident left an imprint on me, too. To this day I am nervous about driving a car into a garage.

On the large back lot, Grandpa operated a veritable truck garden. To the left of the path were neat rows of vegetables—potatoes, onions, and carrots. There were no tomatoes, for he firmly believed that tomatoes were "poison." On the right of the path he planted berry bushes—raspberries, currants, and gooseberries, as well as a healthy strawberry bed. In addition, there was a lovely grape arbor near the house where the vines hung heavy with grapes.

Nothing was ever wasted in this household. Potatoes, carrots, and cabbages were stored in the little black cellar under the pantry. Along improvised shelves in a back room, Grandpa arranged onions to dry for the winter. We seldom ate berries fresh from the bushes. Cream was saved for butter and cooking. Cream soured in a thunderstorm, but was put to good use in the cookies. The berries, cooked in a very light syrup, were put up in quart jars and stored in a separate pantry where the temperature was just right for keeping food without refrigeration. These glass jars of "sauce" accompanied every "company meal" throughout the year. Grapes were an exception. We ate them fresh from the vine and often had a bowlful in the middle of the oilcloth-covered table. But they spoiled rapidly and drew flies, so this was discouraged. I found it delightful to go to the arbor and pick a bunch of amethyst grapes to eat on the spot. As with everything Grandpa cultivated, they grew in profusion; to prevent waste, Grandma cooked some of them into juice, which was brought from the cellar for callers.

Sometimes Aunt Julia came home from Ironwood, Michigan, for a visit. These visits were not the happiest times for her parents. Aunt Julia ran up dressmaking bills. She also scoffed at her mother's Spartan ways and took over much of the baking. No more watery egg-white frostings now. Julia knew how to boil sugar and milk and make fancy fillings between the layers, instead of Grandma's jelly. She skimmed sweet cream from the milk and poured it over rich puddings. She used real butter in the cookies, and crimped her hair with a curling iron heated in the chimney of the dresser lamp. When friends or relatives from Winchester brought gifts of pork or beef that Grandma could stretch for several meals, Julia cooked it all at once. We lived high during her visits. Julia arrived with a barrel of empty glass jars and returned with jars filled with cooked fruits and berries. Grandpa paid the freight.

Editor's Note: Henrietta was the wife of the late Fred Bear, a noted author, adventurer, and manufacturer of archery equipment. They lived in Gainesville, Florida, today the site of the Fred Bear Museum. Her sister, Erna Oleson Xan, co-authored Time-Honored Norwegian Recipes Adapted to the American Kitchen, *first published by Vesterheim.*

Reminiscences

by Hilda Nelson

Recipes didn't really mean much in the Depression. It was a matter of making anything reach as far as possible. I creamed many things because it made them good, and they went much further: for example, peas, tuna or salmon, and potatoes.

If plenty of cooked potatoes were left from dinner, a little meat with onion could be stretched to make a good hash. When this went through the meat grinder, a slice of dry bread was ground last to be sure that no bit of meat remained to go to waste in the grinder.

Even leftover pancakes were not wasted. They were cut in squares the next morning and simmered a bit in rich milk. This was served in soup plates with a sprinkle of sugar for breakfast.

Dessert for dinner was often a bit of leftover fruit sauce of any kind or a pint jar of juice from any fruit or berry, which was thickened with cornstarch and served, of course, with a bit of cream over it.

Salt herring, another standby, was cleaned and then simmered a little in water, drained and simmered next in rich milk or cream. This made wonderful gravy for the potatoes.

Prunes and raisins were the base for sweet soup. I added any bits of fruit and sauce I had. A stick of cinnamon was a must. Wild grape juice made it special. My mother in Norway used lingonberries, but I never had them here. Sometimes I added macaroni to give a richer and thicker soup. It did not change the taste and it increased the amount.

When the church choir practiced, I made them sponge cake with a custard sauce on it. We had the eggs and milk on the farm, so there was nothing to buy.

Editor's Note: Hilda Nelson of Fergus Falls, Minnesota, who was born in Norway, reminisced about cooking on the family farm in Swan Lake Parish, Ottertail County, Minnesota, in the 1920s and 1930s. She was the mother of the late Dr. Marion John Nelson, director of Vesterheim for many years.

The Specialties of Norway

Some Norwegian foods are scarcely ever found outside of the nation. One of these is *gravlaks,* uncooked and marinated salmon. In early times it was put into the ground (into its own "grave"). Today a salmon is covered with salt, sugar, and dill and put under a weight for several days. It is sliced very thin and served chilled as an addition to the smorgasbord.

Reindeer meat is a familiar item on the menu in some Norwegian restaurants. In the days before electric freezers and modern transportation, *spekemat* (cured and dried meats) was a necessity for some remote farm families. Three popular dried meats are *fenalår, spekeskinke,* and *spekekjøtt.* These meats and other dried food were hung in the storehouse, or *stabbur.* Even today, each farmhouse has its own *stabbur. Fenalår* is a leg of lamb that has been soaked in sweetened brine, and then hung in the air to dry. It could be kept for several years. *Spekeskinke* is a ham prepared like *fenalår.* According to legend, *spekeskinke* should be laid away in November and will be ready to eat when the cuckoo returns to Norway and lets out its first call in the spring. Urban housewives now skip the work and buy it ready to serve from the butcher. *Spekekjøtt* is cured dried lamb.

Lutefisk (lyefish) is first soaked in water for several days, then in lye made from birch ash or in a mixture of water and caustic soda, then soaked in water. Any lutefisk fans today are most likely to buy it at the store, ready for boiling in salted water. It can also be purchased in frozen form. Lutefisk is usually served with melted butter and accompanied by boiled potatoes.

Gjetost is a caramel-colored cheese made from goat's milk. It is not widely available in America. Some Wisconsin roadside cheese outlets offer this treat.

Rull is spiced, rolled, and pressed mutton or calf. *Sylte* is headcheese made of pork. Both are traditional on the Christmas smorgasbord.

Cloudberries, or *multer,* are yellow berries that grow wild on mountain plateaus. They are scarce, and whoever finds a patch keeps secret the location. Lingonberries are similar to high bush cranberries in America.

Aquavit *(akevitt)* is a distilled liquor made of potatoes and grain and may be flavored with caraway. The name means "water of life." One Norwegian brand, *Linie,* is so-called because it travels in oak casks aboard cargo ships from Norway to Australia and crosses the "line" (equator). Whether it is the motion of the ship or the change in temperature is not certain, but the long journey is said to improve the flavor. At the table the bottle is often encased in ice. Aquavit is colorless and potent. It must not be diluted with ice cubes or a mix, but is served icy cold in a glass so small that it will be emptied in one gulp. It is usually served with a beer chaser and the beer must never be chilled. Toasting often "opens" the meal. You do not begin eating until the *skål!*

Norwegians tend to eat a hearty breakfast that includes a glass of milk. Unlike the Danes, they do not favor sweets for breakfast. People often take a sandwich to work and carry it into a cafeteria where it is perfectly acceptable to order only coffee. The evening meal is early, from 4:00 to 4:30. Sandwiches or pastry with tea and milk at 9:00 p.m. is customary.

Water and coffee are not usually served with meals. Following the meal, coffee and pastry are served in the living room.

Norwegians' favorite herb is dill, the favorite flavoring almond, and the spice cardamom.

Norway is the longest country in Europe. Food preferences vary tremendously and methods of preparing the same food differ from one valley to another because the mountains tended to bar communication. Wherever you are, in Norway or in a Norwegian-American home, your hostess may say, *"Velkommen til bords"* ("welcome to the table") or *"Vær så god"* ("be so good") when dinner is ready. After dining, you can tell her *"Tusen takk for maten!"* ("a thousand thanks for the food!")

Editor's Note: Many of the recipes in this book were first printed in Notably Norwegian *in 1982. They have become a classic guide for all those who want to cook the traditional Norwegian style. With rare exceptions, biographical data about the contributors with their recipes has not been updated.*

Supplies for Norwegian Cooks

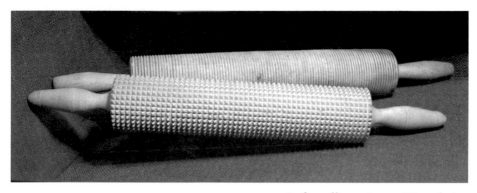

Lefse rolling pins at Vesterheim

Tools

Krumkake electric iron
Krumkake cone-shaped roller
Lefsa grill, rolling pin, and
   turning stick
Heart-shaped waffle iron
Kransekake ring pans (non-stick)
   Each one of 6 pans has 3 rings
   to make 18 different size rings
   for making the ring cake

Rosette-timbale iron. A set
   contains a double handle and 6
   assorted forms (3 rosette and
   3 timbale)
Fattigmann cutter
Goro iron
Sandbakkel tins

Approximate Metric Equivalents

$^1/_4$ teaspoon = 1.23 milliliters
$^1/_2$ teaspoon = 2.46 milliliters
$^3/_4$ teaspoon = 3.7 milliliters
1 teaspoon = 4.93 milliliters
$1^1/_4$ teaspoons = 6.16 milliliters
$1^1/_2$ teaspoons = 7.39 milliliters
$1^3/_4$ teaspoons = 8.63 milliliters
2 teaspoons = 9.86 milliliters
1 tablespoon = 14.79 milliliters
2 tablespoons = 29.57 milliliters

$^1/_4$ cup = 59.15 milliliters
$^1/_2$ cup = 118.3 milliliters
1 cup = 236.59 milliliters
2 cups or 1 pint = 473.18 milliliters
3 cups = 709.77 milliliters
4 cups or 1 quart = 946.36 milliliters
4 quarts or 1 gallon = 3.785 liters

Temperature
To get Celsius (Centigrade) when
Fahrenheit is known: Subtract 32,
multiply by 5, divide by 9.

Skoal

The term *skoal (skål* in Norwegian) is used throughout Scandinavia as a friendly toast. A tale that the word originated when the fierce Vikings drank toasts from the skulls of their dead enemies is at best dubious.

Vesterheim photo

This ale bowl in the Vesterheim collection came to the museum from an immigrant family in Dawson, Minnesota. It is typical of a type found in Voss in western Norway and other areas. The ale bowl with horsehead handles has a prototype in dragon-headed ale bowls of the Middle Ages. The form is near that of the Viking ships, and the name for an early type, kane, *is the same as for a small boat.*

Main Dishes
Meats, Fish, and Dumplings

There is an old Norwegian saying: "If the fish is fresh, boiled is best."

Norwegian immigrants brought these eighteenth-century silver fish servers, sugar spoons, and ale tankard, which are in the Vesterheim collection.

Meatballs
Norma's kjøttboller

Norma Anderson Wangsness of Decorah, Ia., says: "This is our all-time family favorite and always made for Christmas Eve supper. The rest of the menu includes lutefisk, mashed potatoes, baked mashed rutabagas, lefse, flatbread, scalloped corn, a Christmas salad of red and green gelatin or a 24-hour salad, rømmegrøt, *and spritz cookies."*

Meatballs:
- **2 quarts water**
- **1 medium onion, chopped**
- **few stalks celery, finely chopped**
- **1¹/₂ lbs. ground round steak or mix of pork, beef, and veal (preferably unseasoned)**
- **1 cup cream**
- **1 egg**
- **1 Tbsp. cornstarch**
- **salt and pepper (salt optional because of soups used in gravy)**

Gravy:
- **2 cans consommé**
- **1 can cream of mushroom soup**
- **3 Tbsp. flour**

Heat water, onion, and celery in deep kettle. Mix meatball ingredients well and form into balls. When water boils, drop meatballs into liquid and simmer until they hold their shapes. Remove from broth and put meatballs into a baking dish sprayed with vegetable spray. Cover meatballs with soups mixed with flour. Bake at 350 degrees F covered for 1 hour. Uncover and bake ¹/₂ hour more to brown.

"This can be prepared and frozen before baking. Thaw and bake. I usually do 10 pounds of meatball mixture at a time and freeze several assorted size casseroles so I always have a spare for unexpected company. For that amount of meat, use 4 cups cream, seven or eight eggs, 6 to 8 tablespoons cornstarch, eight cans of consommé, eight cans of mushroom soup, and 1 cup flour."

Norwegian Meatballs
Kjøttboller

Olivia Vik Hendrickson of Decorah, Ia., writes: "I grew up in a large family where much food was prepared. Through the years there were times when the budget couldn't include steaks, etc., so this was what we made instead.

"Having been a teacher and the wife of a school administrator, I

have done a great deal of entertaining. These meatballs go well with new peas and potatoes as well as with potato salad. Once the meat is ready, you can entertain at the drop of a hat."

- 1 lb. lean pork
- 1 lb. lean beef
- 2 large potatoes, boiled and mashed, or 1 cup instant potatoes prepared with 1 cup boiling water
- 2 eggs
- 1 cup milk
- 1 small onion, finely chopped

Grind meat finely. (I have my butcher put it through the grinder three times.) Mix all ingredients well. Shape into rolls the size of an egg. Dip balls in flour. Fry in butter or margarine. Put into a 13"x9" pan. Rinse skillet with 1½ cups water. Pour over meatballs. Bake at 325 degrees F for 40 minutes. Turn down temperature to 300 degrees for an additional 20 minutes.

"This will serve six generously. These meatballs freeze well, so can be made ahead. I usually double the recipe. They are a good gift."

Meatballs
Kjøttboller

This recipe is used at the First Lutheran Church Smorgasbord for the Nordic Fest in Decorah, Ia. Notice that no onions are used. According to Norma Wangsness of Decorah, "A real Norwegian never puts onions in meatballs. The consommé and mushroom soup are present-day additions. Also, evaporated milk is substituted for cream as the old-fashioned 'from the farm' cream is not possible to get. For Nordic Fest, the ladies of the Circle would each make a 10-pound batch and deliver it to the church ready to serve. Now they gather at church to make all that will be needed and each lady takes some home to freeze and return at Nordic Fest time."

- 5 lbs. beef, pork, and veal, finely ground
- 6 Tbsp. salt (optional)
- 1 tsp. dry mustard
- 1 tsp. mace
- 1 tsp. pepper
- 1½ 13-oz. cans evaporated milk
- 1 can consommé
- 1 can mushroom soup

Mix meat, salt, mustard, mace, pepper, and milk. Form into balls.

Brown in butter. Add mixture of soups. Simmer briefly. Place in casserole and bake at 350 degrees F for 1 hour.

Royal Pot Roast
Slottsstek

Verla Williams of Iowa City, Iowa

- **2 Tbsp. butter**
- **2 Tbsp. vegetable oil**
- **4 lbs. boneless beef (round, rump, or chuck)**
- **1 cup finely chopped onion**
- **3 Tbsp. flour**
- **1 Tbsp. dark corn syrup**
- **2 Tbsp. white vinegar**
- **2 cups beef stock**
- **1 large bay leaf**
- **6 flat anchovy fillets, washed and drained**
- **1 tsp. whole peppercorns, crushed and tied in cheesecloth**
- **salt**
- **black pepper, freshly ground**

In heavy 5- to 6-quart oven-proof casserole melt butter and oil over moderate heat. When foam subsides, brown meat on all sides, taking about 15 minutes. Remove meat from pan. Add onion and cook over moderately high heat 6 to 8 minutes, stirring occasionally until lightly browned. Remove pan from heat. Add flour. Stir gently to blend. Add dark syrup, white vinegar, and stock. Add bay leaf, anchovies, and bag of peppercorns. Replace meat, cover, and bring to boil on top of stove. Preheat oven to 350 degrees F. Place casserole on shelf in lower third of oven, regulating heat so liquid barely simmers. Meat should be tender in about 3 hours.

Transfer roast to heated platter. Cover with foil to keep warm. Discard bay leaf and peppercorns. Skim off surface fat. Taste and add salt and pepper if necessary. If flavor is lacking, boil briskly, uncovered, over high heat to concentrate. Pour in gravy boat and serve with meat.

"In Scandinavia, *slottsstek* is usually accompanied by red currant jelly or lingonberries, and often with gherkins and boiled potatoes."

Vacations

July is Norway's vacation month with most businesses closed for at least three weeks.

Pressed Sandwich Meat
Rullepølse

Barbara Hawes of Grand Rapids, Mich., writes, "This meat roll recipe was given to me by my Norwegian friends, William and Birdene Amundson of Grand Rapids, who formerly lived in Stoughton, Wis. It is a challenge to make, but worth it." Barbara's interests include rosemaling, cooking, and quilting.

2$^1/_2$ lbs. beef flank
1 Tbsp. pepper
4 tsp. salt
2 tsp. ginger
$^1/_2$ tsp. sugar
1 lb. thinly sliced beef from the round
$^1/_2$ lb. sliced pork tenderloin
$^1/_4$ lb. finely ground pork
$^1/_4$ lb. finely ground beef
3 Tbsp. minced onion

Trim all fat from flank. Flatten with meat pounder on a board. Mix seasonings, spice, and sugar. Rub part of mixture into flank. Place sliced beef and pork on half of flank. Combine ground beef and pork with remaining seasonings and onion. Spread over beef and pork slices.

Roll meat tightly; sew together with strong thread. Wrap tightly in a piece of cheesecloth. Put into a heavy kettle and cover with water. Simmer for 2$^1/_2$ to 3 hours until tender.

Remove from kettle. Place roll between two heavy plates under a heavy weight to press out moisture. Keep in cool place several hours or overnight. Remove cloth and thread. Refrigerate.

Serve cold, cut in thin slices. Makes 10 to 12 servings. Can be made ahead. "A fine addition to a buffet menu."

Norwegian Taco
Lefsekling

Eunice Stoen of Decorah sent this recipe. She says: "This was the result of trying to come up with a unique food to serve during Decorah's Nordic Fest. My good friend Ida Sacquitne tells us her grandmother called it lefsekling *whenever they wrapped whatever they had to eat in lefse. Most Norwegians don't like too hot a sauce, so we mixed one part of the mild taco sauce to two parts catsup."*

Meat mixture:
chopped onion
butter
ground beef
salt and pepper

3 to 4 Tbsp. brown sugar
chicken gumbo soup
Filling ingredients:
    shredded head lettuce
    chopped tomatoes
    white cheese, shredded in
        food processor
    chopped onions
    mild sauce, 2 parts catsup to
        1 part taco sauce
    lefse (about 9" size)

Brown onion in butter; add beef and brown. Add salt and pepper to taste, a little brown sugar, and $\frac{1}{2}$ to 1 can chicken gumbo soup, depending on amount of meat. Simmer and keep warm for serving.

To serve: With the lefse as the base, put handful of lettuce on top, then 2 or 3 tablespoons meat, tomatoes, cheese, onion, and sauce. Fold up and then fold in sides, and then fold the top down and serve in square of foil along with two or three paper napkins. "Very tasty, but messy to eat."

Make small 9-inch lefse for this recipe. About $\frac{1}{6}$ cup dough will make that size.

Remoulade Sandwich
Rulade smørbrød

The recipe for this sandwich, served at the Nordic Brunch and dinner, comes from Berit Gjerde of Edina, Minn. The two meals are sponsored annually by the Twin Cities Friends of the Norwegian-American Museum.

For each sandwich, stack in the following order:
    1 well-buttered slice whole
        wheat bread
    1 leaf Bibb lettuce, washed,
        dried, and pressed down
    2 slices roast beef, placed flat
        with an overlapped twist
    2 Tbsp. chopped soft fried
        onion, tucked under
        rounded form of beef
        slices
$1\frac{1}{2}$ Tbsp. Remoulade sauce
    3 slices pickled beets
    1 tsp. parsley, snipped and
        sprinkled over surface
    3 thin cucumber slices, cut
        and twisted to crown top
Remoulade Sauce:
    1 egg
    1 Tbsp. lemon juice
$\frac{3}{4}$ tsp. salt
$\frac{1}{2}$ tsp. dry mustard
$\frac{1}{4}$ tsp. paprika
$\frac{1}{8}$ tsp. ground white pepper

1 cup salad oil, divided
1 Tbsp. lemon juice
$^1/_2$ tsp. garlic salt
2 tsp. anchovy paste
1 sprig parsley
4 stuffed green olives
1 tsp. chervil

Have all ingredients at room temperature. Put egg, the first tablespoon lemon juice, salt, dry mustard, paprika, and pepper into blender. Cover and run on low speed. While blender is running, slowly pour in $^1/_2$ cup salad oil.

When more power is needed, turn speed to high and add second tablespoon lemon juice. Slowly add remaining half cup salad oil.

If the mixture separates, pour it into bowl. Wash and dry blender container. Break one egg into container, cover, and run on low speed. While blender is running slowly, add the separated mixture until it is the desired thickness.

Add garlic salt, anchovy paste, parsley, green olives, and chervil. Blend. Refrigerate until ready to use. Makes 1$^1/_4$ cups, enough for 16 sandwiches.

> *Please be aware of the danger of eating raw egg.*

Kirsten Flagstad's Favorite Sandwich

Opera lovers for many years enjoyed Kirsten Flagstad through the Metropolitan Opera radio broadcasts. Born in 1895, she came from a musical family and made her debut in the Oslo National Theatre at age 18. She was known for her Wagnerian roles as Brunnhilde and Isolde. In 1959, she was a founder and the first director of the Norway Opera in Oslo. This recipe is reprinted with permission from Forlaget Tanum-Norli A/S of Oslo, publisher of Norway's Delight *by Elise Sverdup.*

$^1/_2$ ox kidney
flour
salt and pepper
butter
1 cup cream
1 glass sherry
4 slices milk loaf
celeriac
baked apple
tomato and parsley for
  garnish

Cut up kidney into small cubes; dust with flour, salt, and pepper and brown in butter. Add cream and sherry and simmer for 5 minutes.

Remove crusts from four slices of milk loaf and fry in butter.

Place one round lightly boiled disc of celeriac on each slice, then a warm, thick slice of baked apple. Spoon the kidney on top of each loaf and garnish with tomato and parsley. Serves 4.

Pork Sandwich Filling
Flesk pålegg

Esther M. Johnson, Ossian, Iowa, writes: "My mother's maiden name was Stena Tofte Anderson. Tofte, Minn., on Lake Superior, was named for my grandfather and his brother.

"Later my grandfather came south to Dover township, Fayette County, Iowa. Taking his father's first name which was Anders and adding 'on,' it became Anderson, so he went by Hans Tofte Anderson."

  3- to 4-lb. pork roast
  2 medium onions
  1 10^1/$_2$-oz. can cream of
      chicken soup

Boil roast in unsalted water until tender. Grind with onions. Mix with soup. If the roast is large, two cans of soup may be needed.

  This will make enough filling for at least 2 dozen double sandwiches. Freezes well.

Norwegian Stew
Lapskaus

Josefa Hansen Andersen of Chicago, Ill., writes that in Chicago this is often served on May 17, Norway's Independence Day. "At one time," she says, "There were more than forty churches in Chicago with services in Norwegian, but now there is only one." That is her church, the Norwegian Lutheran Memorial Church, 2612 North Kedzie Boulevard.

  1^1/$_2$ cups diced uncooked beef
  ^{1}/$_2$ cup diced uncooked pork
  1 onion, diced
  1^1/$_2$ cups diced, cooked corned
      beef
  4 cups diced raw potatoes
  ^{1}/$_2$ tsp. pepper

Cover beef and pork with water and boil slowly for half an hour. Add remaining ingredients and cook until tender.

Muriel Humphrey's Beef Soup
Kjøttsuppe

Muriel Humphrey Brown of Waverly, Minn., was the wife of the late Hubert Humphrey, vice-president of the United States from 1965-1969. She says: "This is a hearty old family recipe my father used to make and was Hubert's favorite. He liked to tell everyone it gave him vim, vigor, and vitality. Makes six good, hearty bowls."

1½ lbs. stew beef or chuck
plus soup bone
1 tsp. salt
½ tsp. pepper
2 bay leaves
4 or 5 medium carrots,
sliced
½ cup chopped onion
1 cup chopped celery
1 cup chopped cabbage
1 1-lb. can Italian-style
tomatoes
1 Tbsp. Worcestershire sauce
1 beef bouillon cube
pinch oregano or other spice

Cover meat with cold water in heavy 3-quart kettle. Add salt, pepper, and bay leaves. Bring to bubbly stage while preparing vegetables. Turn heat low and add carrots, onion, celery, and cabbage. Simmer at least 2½ hours or until meat is very tender.

Remove bone and bay leaves. Cut meat into bite-sized pieces. Add tomatoes, Worcestershire sauce, bouillon cube, and spices. Simmer for ½ hour longer and serve.

"This recipe is especially good for a light supper meal with fruit salad, a glass of milk, lots of crackers and dessert. It is low in calories, but high in food value."

Potato Dumplings and Roast Rork
Kumla med svinesteik

Marilyn Skaugstad of Iowa City

4- to 5-lb pork roast
Dumplings:
5 lbs. raw potatoes, peeled
and grated
1 Tbsp. salt
2 to 2½ cups flour

Cook pork roast in salted water for about 2 hours to make tasty broth. Grate potatoes and drain excess moisture. Add salt and 2 cups flour to make dumpling dough. Mix well and test a tablespoon of dough in slowly boiling broth. If it falls apart, add another ½ cup flour to dough and test again until it stays together. Drop gently by large tablespoons into the slowly boiling broth. Dip spoon in broth between dumplings. Cover and cook about 1 to 1½ hours. Occasionally shake pan to prevent sticking to bottom of pan. Serve hot with butter to accompany the pork roast. Makes about 16 large dumplings.

Salt Pork (Side Pork) and Gravy
Sideflesk

Dagny Stenehjem Padilla, Minnetonka, Minn., writes: "My great-great-grandparents and great-grandparents used this recipe for a hearty breakfast when they pioneered southeastern Minnesota in 1849. My folks used it occasionally when I was growing up. It's an economical and filling meal."

1 lb. side pork, sliced
flour
milk
bread
sugar

Brown slices of pork and put aside. Pour off fat, reserving about 2 tablespoons. Mix fat and about 4 tablespoons flour. Over medium heat, gradually add milk, stirring to keep lumps from forming. Let come to a boil to thicken gravy. Serve gravy over a slice of bread. Sprinkle sugar over gravy. Serve with cooked pork slices.

Carving by Phillip Odden

Lamb in Cabbage
Får i kål

Mrs. Josefa Hansen Andersen of Chicago, Ill., writes, "I was born in Mandal, Norway, and came with my parents to the United States when I was a few months old. My parents owned the largest Norwegian restaurant in this country from 1915 to 1932 so I was raised in the food environment."
When Mrs. Andersen and her husband visited Norway several years ago, they found it impossible to purchase lamb because Princess Astrid was entertaining friends on her yacht and had purchased all the local lamb in Fredrikstad.
"Knowing the butcher, my husband was successful in obtaining lamb so we could have får i kål. *Saint Hans Day, June 24, is the longest day of the year.* Får i kål *is often served with boiled potatoes at gatherings on Saint Hans Day."*

3 lbs. lamb stew meat, cut in
**   3-inch cubes**
1 cabbage, cut in 8 wedges
3 tsp. salt
1 Tbsp. whole peppercorns
¹/₄ cup flour
¹/₄ cup water

In a heavy pot, alternately layer cubes of lamb and wedges of cabbage. Sprinkle with salt. Place peppercorns in two cheesecloth bags and add to pot. Add water until it breaks to the surface of the top layer of meat. Simmer for 1½ hours or until meat is fork tender.

Remove bags of peppercorns and gently move layered stew to one side of the pot. Thicken stock with a mixture of flour and water. Gravy will be light in color since no frying has taken place. Rearrange stew into original position. Serves 5 or 6.

Lamb in Cabbage
Får i kål

This recipe comes from Birgitte Christianson of Decorah, Ia., who was born in Copenhagen and whose husband teaches at Luther College and is assistant director for the academic affairs of the Norwegian-American Museum. "This is a traditional Norwegian dish, served both in the country and in the city in Norway. Many Norwegian-Americans are not aware of how much lamb and mutton are used in Norway. We have been served this old-fashioned and hearty dish in friends' homes there."

3 to 4 lbs. lamb, trimmed of all fat and cut into 1½-inch cubes
3 Tbsp. butter or margarine
½ cup flour
pepper to taste, about 2 tsp.
1 large onion, sliced
2 lbs. white cabbage, coarsely sliced
2 Tbsp. salt, approximately
3 cups chicken broth

Brown lamb cubes in butter over medium heat a few at a time until evenly and nicely browned. Remove from pan as they are browned and place in a large bowl. Sprinkle meat with flour and toss until all pieces are well-coated and all flour has disappeared. Pepper to taste.

In 6-quart ovenproof casserole layer lamb cubes, onion slices, and cabbage slices, using half the ingredients each time. Salt each layer lightly. End with layer of cabbage.

Pour fat out of pan used to brown meat. Add chicken broth and boil, scraping browned meat residue from bottom of pan. Pour broth over meat and vegetables. Bake at 350 degrees F 1½ to 2 hours or until meat is tender. Serves 6. This is good with parsleyed boiled potatoes. It can be made ahead and reheated.

Cabbage Balls
Kål boller

Betty Nelson Seegmiller of Decorah, Ia., is a former administrative assistant at Vesterheim.

1 15-oz. can sauerkraut
1 10 ³/₄-oz. can tomato soup
regular rice
1 8-oz. pkg. lightly seasoned
    pork sausage
cabbage leaves

Combine sauerkraut, tomato soup, and one can water in heavy saucepan. (I prefer a large cast-iron kettle.) Bring to boil and simmer gently. Mix equal volumes of rice and pork sausage. Put 1 tablespoon mixture on cabbage leaf, roll up, and secure with string or toothpicks. Place cabbage balls in pot with sauerkraut and tomato soup mixture and simmer gently for about 4 hours. Check occasionally to see that there is enough liquid so mixture will not burn. Serves 6 to 8.

"For ease in handling cabbage leaves, put the whole head in a small amount of boiling water and allow to cook just enough to peel off a leaf at a time without breaking it."

Norwegian Fish Balls
Fiskeboller

Violet D. Christophersen of Marinette, Wis., was one of the first three rosemalers to win a Gold Medal. She writes: "Directions for this dish are given exactly the way it was taught to me many years ago. During the time-consuming process of preparing the fish balls, we dressed warm and worked in a cold room in order to keep the fresh fish from any possible spoilage."

2 quarts whole milk
2 dozen fresh herring or
    blue fins
4 small raw potatoes, peeled
¹/₃ cup soft butter, not melted
3 eggs, lightly beaten
¹/₄ tsp. mace
¹/₄ tsp. nutmeg
    salt and pepper to taste

Scald milk. Set aside to chill thoroughly. Scale fish, then clean. Remove the skin. Scrape off any meat adhering to the skin. Remove all bones.

Put all bones and skin into a kettle, add enough salted water to cover, and let boil 10 minutes. Strain. Add enough water to the strained liquid to fill kettle half full. This liquid will be used to boil the fish balls in.

Grind the scraped fish through a meat grinder together with the peeled raw potatoes three to five times. Put well-ground fish into an extra large mixing bowl. With the help of a wooden potato masher, use a pounding and mashing effect on the ground fish until it forms tough dough. (An electric beater works well, too.) Add the soft butter and continue mashing. Add beaten eggs and the chilled milk, a cup at a time, with much pounding and mashing in between. Add the spices and seasoning to taste, being careful not to add too much spice. A delicate flavor is desired.

When the mass is light and fluffy, with a tablespoon first dipped in cold water and then dipped into fish batter, drop like dumplings into the boiling fish broth. Let boil until done, about 7 or 8 minutes. The fish balls will rise to the surface when done.

Put fish balls into an earthen crock and pour the fish stock over all. It will keep for several weeks in a cold place. Or, you may pack some of the fish balls into sterilized jars, adding some of the liquid in which they were boiled. Seal jars and cook in hot water bath for 1 hour.

To serve, fry fish balls in butter until delicately browned.

Variation: Make a boiled white sauce seasoned with salt and pepper and pour over fish balls.

Company Fish Balls in White Sauce
Selskaps fiskeboller i hvitsaus

Barbara Hamre Berg of Decorah, Ia., studied weaving in Fagernes, Norway, at the Valdres Husflidskole. At Iowa State University she was in an Honors Program Project in Scandinavian Design. She is a freelance designer of both interiors and Scandinavian crafts. She says: "This dish was served to my husband and me when we visited cousins in Drammen, Norway. It was served over thin, shell-shaped pastries. A cucumber salad was also served."

1 14-oz. can fish balls
1/2 cup butter
1/2 cup flour
1 13-oz. can evaporated milk
    fresh milk
1 6-oz. pkg. frozen shrimp, thawed, cooked, and peeled
1 10-oz. pkg. frozen peas, thawed
1/4 tsp. dill weed
salt and pepper to taste

Drain fish balls, reserving liquid. Quarter fish balls and set aside. Melt butter in saucepan, add flour, and cook until well-blended. Combine the fish liquid, evaporated milk, and fresh milk to make 3 cups. Stir into butter-flour mixture and cook until smooth and hot.

Add the fish balls, shrimp, and peas. Cook until heated through. Add the dill, salt, and pepper. If too thick, add a little hot milk. Serve with puff pastry shells or with boiled potatoes. "There are never any leftovers."

Fish Balls in Curry
Fiskeboller i karrisaus

Eva Lund Haugen, who was born in Kongsvinger, Norway, sent this recipe. Her husband, Einar Haugen, is professor emeritus of Scandinavian and Linguistics at Harvard University. For thirty-three years he was chairman of Scandinavian studies at the University of Wisconsin. He is a member of the Board of Directors of the Norwegian-American Museum. Dr. Marion Nelson, museum director, suggested this fish ball recipe since he had enjoyed the dish in the Haugen home.

3 Tbsp. butter
3 Tbsp. flour
2 tsp. curry powder
$1/2$ cup fish stock, fish bouillon, or chicken stock
$1^{1}/_{2}$ cups milk
1 16-oz. can Norwegian fish balls

Melt butter in a heavy-bottomed three-quart saucepan. Add flour and curry to melted butter. Stir for 2 minutes. Add stock and stir well. Add milk, stirring constantly. Simmer 10 minutes. Add fish balls and heat through on low heat. Serves three or four.

"If you wish to make it ahead, it can be reheated. It is normally served with boiled or steamed potatoes, green peas, and carrots. Instead of fish balls, you can use cooked boneless and skinless fish. Instead of curry, you could use 2 tablespoons drained capers which should be added before the simmering stage. This is a common everyday dish. We like a strong curry; you may want a bit less."

Sardines

Sardines caught in the summer are better than those caught in the winter. Called summer Brislings, they are usually packed in olive oil. Sild, or winter Brislings, are packed in soya oil or tomato or mustard sauce.

Lutefisk

Hyla Beroen Lehman of Cedar Rapids, Iowa, is a performing artist, lecturer, and educator, "one hundred percent Norwegian by descent. Olaf Glosemodt, my father's great uncle, was a famed Norwegian sculptor in the nineteenth century, a contemporary of Ibsen and Grieg. In 1872, he carved from one solid block of marble the crowning chair used in the coronation of King Oscar in Christiania (later Oslo).

"On Christmas Eve, lutefisk is traditionally served in our home with buttered lefse, boiled potatoes, cranberries or lingonberries, and a green vegetable. Dessert features an elegant tray of assorted Christmas cookies, fruitcake, and festive confections of all kinds. Coffee, of course!"

2 lbs. lutefisk
^{1}/$_2$ lb. butter, melted

Rinse fish thoroughly in cold water. Cut in pieces of serving size. Remove scales from any skin that you have not removed. If desired, tie fish in cheesecloth for cooking since it is very tender and will break apart. Place in cool salted water in 4- or 5-quart saucepan and bring to a boil. Cook for approximately 10 minutes or until tender and translucent. Remove gently and serve with generous amounts of melted butter. Serves four.

Cod Chowder
Torsk

Louise Fladager Sundet of Excelsior, Minn., writes: "My great grandfather, Mons Fladager, came to Spring Grove, Minn., from Valdres, Norway, in 1859. He purchased land and built a two-story frame building which became a general store. My father celebrated the 100th anniversary of the store, then in the family for three generations. Had I been born a boy, I would probably have been living in Spring Grove selling clothes in my father's store!" Mrs. Sundet is a board member of the Norwegian-American Museum.

1 cup chopped onion
1/4 cup butter
4 cups diced raw potato
2 tsp. salt
1/2 tsp. coarsely ground black
    pepper
2 cups water
1 lb. frozen cod, partially
    thawed, cut in cubes
1 17-oz. can whole kernel
    corn, undrained
1 13-oz. can evaporated milk

In a large kettle, sauté onion in butter. Add potato, seasonings, and water. Cover and simmer 15 minutes. Put cod on top of potatoes. Cover and simmer an additional 15 minutes. Stir in undrained corn and evaporated milk. Cover and heat to just below the boiling point.

"I sprinkle some parsley flakes on top to give it a little color!"

Poached Salmon
Kokt laks

Caron Gunnerud, St. Paul, Minn. This dish was served at the Nordic Brunch and Dinner fund-raiser for the Norwegian-American Museum in Decorah, Ia.

1 gallon water
1 cup salt

2 lbs. fresh salmon, cut in
    slices
lemon wedges and parsley

Bring water and salt to boil. Add fish. Allow to simmer 12 to 15 minutes. Skim carefully to prevent gray film from forming on the fish. Serve salmon on a hot platter. Garnish with lemon wedges and parsley. Serves six.

Fish Soup
Fiskesuppe

Sigurd Daasvand of Oslo

fish stock
2 carrots, sliced
1 parsnip, diced
1 stalk celery, sliced
green peas (optional)
1 heaping Tbsp. flour
1 cup top milk or cream
1 Tbsp. chopped chives or
    parsley
1 egg or 1/2 cup cream
1/2 tsp. vinegar and 1/2 tsp.
    sugar or 1 tsp. sweet
    relish (optional)

Use the skimmed stock obtained from boiling fish heads, skin, and bones, when the rest of the fish is used for something else, or use the stock from canned fish balls, or use the water in which fish has been boiled the previous day. In this stock boil the sliced carrots, diced parsnip, celery, and perhaps a few green peas. When vegetables are tender, thicken soup with flour stirred with top milk or cream. After simmering for 10 minutes or more, add chopped chives or parsley.

Place egg, or a little cream, in the soup tureen and pour soup in while beating vigorously.

Some people like a little sour taste added to this soup. To obtain this flavor, a half teaspoon each of vinegar and sugar, a little sweet pickling syrup, or sweet relish may be added after removing soup from heat. But it is better that each person adds this to his or her taste, rather than to add it to the whole amount.

If fish balls are on hand, by all means add them to the soup after it has been thickened. Serve two or three in each soup plate. Diced potatoes and other vegetables may also be used.

Dumplings in Milk Soup
Melkesuppe med boller

Dr. Marion Nelson, former director of the Norwegian-American Museum in Decorah, sends this recipe. It comes from his mother,

Hilda Nelson of Fergus Falls, Minn., who was born in Aalesund in western Norway and emigrated to the United States from Lillehammer in 1903. She, in turn, got it from her mother, Maren Hagen Bergerson. Marion describes himself as "a farm boy from an immigrant family near Fergus Falls, Minn."

Soup:
   1¹/₂ **cups milk**
   1 **tsp. sugar**
   ¹/₄ **tsp. salt**
Dumplings:
   1 **egg**
   ¹/₂ **tsp. sugar**
   ¹/₈ **tsp. salt**
   scant ¹/₈ **tsp. nutmeg**
   1 **tsp. vegetable oil**
   ¹/₂ **cup flour, approximately**
   1 **Tbsp. butter or margarine**

Combine soup ingredients in a 1¹/₂-quart saucepan (an enamel pan is good; a cast-iron enamel pan is even better). Heat to boiling.

While milk is heating prepare dumplings. Break egg into an ample-sized coffee cup, beating lightly with a fork. Add sugar, salt, nutmeg, and oil. Add flour, beating until dough leaves the edge of the cup.

Using 2 teaspoons, pick up a ball of dough a scant teaspoonful in size and drop into slowly simmering milk. Lightly stir occasionally to prevent dumplings from settling to bottom. Simmer until dumplings have doubled in size, about 5 minutes. Add butter or margarine, allowing it to melt. Serve in soup bowls. Makes about 15 dumplings or two moderate servings.

"These dumplings are supposed to be quite firm. A salty meat such as dried beef is a good accompaniment."

Potato Dumplings
Potet klubb

Doris Hagen Campbell of Rochester, Minn. She is a director of the National Bygdelag and Vesterheim.

- ¹/₂ **lb. salt pork**
- **6 cups grated potatoes**
- **4 cups flour**
- **2 tsp. salt**

Cut salt pork into small cubes. Mix potatoes, flour, and salt. Form this mixture into a 3- to 4-inch oval ball, placing a piece of salt pork in the center.

Place in boiling water and cook gently for 1¹/₂ hours.

"My family likes the *klubb* cooked with a ham, or if we can find corned beef without garlic, that also makes a flavorful dish.

"My grandmother from Sigdal taught my mother this family favorite. Now I have taught my daughters-in-law. When we fix *klubb,* I use a restaurant-size soup kettle and triple the recipe.

"The next day I slice the *klubb* and fry it in butter. My family always makes sure there is enough *klubb* left over for this follow-up."

A *potet klubb* recipe was also sent to us from Dorothy Norby of Mabel, Minn., who writes, "My grandmother always served this on Christmas Eve and it is a 'must' in our family every year."

Right: His Royal Highness Haakon, Crown Prince of Norway, dedicated the Amdal-Odland Heritage Center at the Vesterheim Museum, Decorah, Iowa, in 1999. He is shown here with Vesterheim Executive Director Janet Blohm Pultz. The center is decorated in Norwegian folk art by Sigmund Aarseth. H.M. Harold V, King of Norway, is Honorary Chair of Vesterheim's Board of Trustees.

The Norwegian royal family has a long and close relationship with Vesterheim going back over fifty years. In 1939, the then-Crown Prince Olav and Crown Princess Martha visted Vesterheim and presented a gift of Norwegian museum artifacts. Vesterheim photo

Norwegian Dumpling
Norsk klubb

Helen A. Falskerud Pilgrim of Decorah, Iowa. "This recipe was brought over from Norway by my mother."

1 quart milk
1 Tbsp. salt
1¹/₂ cups graham or whole wheat flour
3 cups white flour

In a large bowl put milk, salt, and graham or whole wheat flour. Stir well and add white flour until mixture forms a large ball like bread dough. Cut or pull off a piece of dough baseball size or larger and shape into a small loaf of bread. Heat a large kettle of water to boiling. Drop loaves into boiling water and boil for 1¹/₂ hours or until done when tested with a fork. An aluminum pie pan can be placed in bottom of kettle to keep *klubb* from sticking.

When done, take *klubb* out of kettle and cool. Slice in thin slices and fry in butter or margarine. Top with syrup. Or, instead of frying slices of *klubb,* half-and-half can be poured over slices.

"Good with fried bacon, ham, sausages, or most any kind of meat. Makes about four loaves. They freeze well and can be reheated."

Salads and More

In Norway, salads did not develop as part of the national cuisine. The ingredients just weren't available, according to Marion Nelson, former director of Vesterheim. "Carrots and cabbage are served around meat dishes rather than as a separate dish," he said. The special salad recipes following are favorites of the Norwegian-American contributors.

Vesterheim photo

Birchroot carrying baskets for all imaginable household purposes are in the Vesterheim collection. The small object is for lump sugar. The large baskets were for carrying foods. The simple covered basket (center, back) came to this country with the family of Knute Nelson, renowned governor and senator of Minnesota, at the beginning of the twentieth century.

Cucumber Salad

Marilyn Skaugstad, Iowa City, Iowa

- **8 large cucumbers (European)**
- **$^1/_3$ cup sugar**
- **1 tsp. salt**
- **$^1/_8$ tsp. pepper**
- **2 tbsp. water**
- **$^3/_4$ cup white wine vinegar**
- **1 tbsp. chopped fresh dill or**
  1 tsp. dried dill weed

Peel cucumbers. Slice thinly (should be translucent) by hand or food processor. Pat with paper towels; transfer to large bowl. Combine remaining ingredients, except dill weed, and pour over cucumbers. Cover and chill overnight. Just before serving, drain cucumbers and garnish with dill. Makes 25 servings, about 15 calories per $^1/_4$ cup.

Pickled Beets
Rødbeter

Mary Holum of Minneapolis provided the hotel chef with her recipe for pickled beets for the 1980 Nordic Brunch and Nordic Dinner in Minneapolis, sponsored by Twin Cities Friends of the Norwegian-American Museum.

$^1/_2$ **cup white vinegar**
$^1/_2$ **cup sugar**
  1 1-lb. can sliced beets, including juice
$^1/_2$ **to 1 tsp. salt**
  pepper to taste
  whole cloves (optional)

In a $1^1/_2$- to 2-quart saucepan combine vinegar, sugar, juice from beets, salt, and pepper. A few whole cloves tied in a cloth bag can be added, if desired. Bring to a boil, briskly for 2 minutes.
Place sliced beets in a deep glass, stainless steel or enamel bowl. Pour hot marinade over beets and let them cool, uncovered. When mixture reaches room temperature, cover bowl with plastic wrap; refrigerate at least 12 hours.

Kitchen at the Egge log cabin, 1850s, Vesterheim Norwegian-American Museum Open Air Division

Cranberry Catsup
Tyttebær ketchup

Esther M. Johnson, Ossian, Iowa

  1 lb. cranberries
$^1/_2$ **cup mild vinegar**
$^2/_3$ **cup water**
  1 cup brown sugar
$^1/_2$ **tsp. cloves**
$^1/_2$ **tsp. ginger**
$^1/_2$ **tsp. paprika**
  1 tsp. cinnamon
$^1/_2$ **tsp. salt**
$^1/_4$ **tsp. pepper**
  2 Tbsp. butter

Put cranberries, vinegar, and water in pan and boil until berries are soft (about 5 minutes). Put through a food mill. Add the brown sugar, spices and seasoning and simmer three minutes. Add the butter. Serve at room temperature.

"Cranberry catsup can be refrigerated for months. It's great on roast pork or turkey."

Vesterheim photo

Cranberry Salad

Adella Askvig Valen, wife of the Rev. Elmer Valen, who serves as visitation pastor on the staff of First Lutheran Church in Decorah, Ia., sent this recipe.

"This recipe should serve seven or eight people. It is a very simple salad and can be made ahead of time. It is very good with a turkey or chicken dinner and has always been a favorite of our children . . . When unable to come home, they have been known to telephone from faraway places to check on ingredients and method of preparation."

3 cups thick cranberry sauce
²/₃ cup graham cracker crumbs
¹/₂ pint whipping cream, whipped sugar
¹/₂ tsp. vanilla

Make cranberry sauce with your usual recipe, perhaps using a little less water to make it thicker. Save a few whole cranberries for garnish.

Sweeten whipped cream to taste and add vanilla. Layer cranberry sauce, crumbs, and whipped cream in a clear glass bowl, repeating in same order.

Herring Pâté
Sildepâté

Ruth Wickney, Northwood, N.D.

1 12-oz. jar herring in cream or wine sauce, drained
1 8-oz. pkg. cream cheese
¹/₂ cup pitted ripe olives
¹/₃ cup chopped parsley
¹/₄ to ¹/₂ tsp. curry powder
juice of half a lemon

Place all ingredients in blender and process at highest speed until smooth. Place mixture in a crock and chill. Excellent on party rye with chopped olives and hard-cooked egg garnish. It can also be used with raw vegetables.

Sweet-Sour Cabbage
Surkål

Josefa Hansen Andersen of Chicago

1 head cabbage
1 tsp. salt
2 Tbsp. sugar
¹/₄ cup vinegar
2 Tbsp. caraway seed

Shred cabbage very fine. Add other ingredients. Cover with water and simmer for 2 to 3 hours. Good served with roast pork.

Breads

Above: *Ida Sacquitne makes lefse at Vesterheim. She demonstrated lefse making at the Smithsonian in 1975.*

Left: *A lefse sculpture by Harley Refsal, noted woodcarver, is in the Vesterheim collection. A Luther College professor and author, he has exhibited widely. He also teaches the Scandinavian-style flat-plane carving.*

Lefse
Lefse

*Ida Sacquitne of Decorah, Ia.,
demonstrated lefse-making at the
Norwegian-American Museum in
Decorah and annually for the
Nordic Fest. She also demonstrated
at the Smithsonian Folk Life
Festival in Washington, D.C., in
1975. Her father came to Decorah
with his parents at age 8 from Voss.
"Hard times in Norway caused
them to make the move."*

**5 well-packed cups riced
potatoes
$^1/_2$ cup margarine
3 Tbsp. powdered sugar
2 cups flour
1 tsp. salt**

Use Idaho russet potatoes. Boil,
then mash and rice potatoes. Add
margarine while potatoes are still
warm. Cool until room
temperature.

Add powdered sugar, flour, and
salt. Mix with your hands. Knead
well and then roll into a log.

Cut and measure into $^1/_3$-cup
portions and make a round ball of
each portion. Press it down by
hand and it will be easier to keep
round while rolling out.

Dust the large canvas-like cloth
lefse "board" with flour. Press
dough down, turn over, and press
down again. Roll as thin as
possible with a rolling pin with a
pastry sleeve into large 14-inch
circles to fit lefse grill. The secret
of making *thin* lefse is using a
covered rolling pin. The last roll
across the dough use a grooved
lefse rolling pin, which marks the
dough slightly and makes it
thinner.

Use a lefse stick and roll dough
on stick and transfer to lefse grill.
You must use a lefse stick or holes
will be made in the dough. Bake
on hot lefse grill or a griddle. Bake
a minute or two, then turn with a
lefse stick. Turn when bubbles and
brown spots appear. Fold each
lefse in half or quarters. Cool
between towels and store in plastic
bag. Makes about 18.

Spread with butter to eat. Some
people sprinkle brown or white
sugar on it. Roll up.

"Uff Da"

"Uff da" is an expression widely
used by Americans of Norwegian
descent. It can be translated many
ways, but "Oh, dear" is close. "Uff
da" is to a Norwegian what "Good
grief" is to Charlie Brown. A joke
in some Norwegian communities
has it that "uff da" is being served
Swedish meatballs at a lutefisk
dinner.

Hardanger Lefse
Haringkake

Marilyn Skaugstad, Iowa City

3 pkgs. dry yeast
1 cup warm potato water
6 cups milk, scalded
1 cup sugar
³/₄ cup vegetable shortening
**   or lard**
1 Tbsp. salt
4 cups graham flour
9 to 10 cups all-purpose
**   flour**

Soften yeast in warm potato water 5 to 10 minutes. To scalded milk add sugar, shortening, and salt. Let cool. Combine yeast with milk and add graham flour. Beat mixture until smooth. Let set until it makes soft sponge, about 1 hour. Add enough flour to make soft dough. Put dough in greased bowl; turn over to grease surface. Cover and let rise in warm place until double.

Shape into small buns about the size of an egg and let rise on greased sheets. Roll out thinly, first using lefse rolling pin and then using the special *Haringkake* rolling pin. Use plenty of flour to keep dough from sticking to board. Fold over clean stick and transfer sheet of dough to electric lefse plate and bake at low setting until browned on both sides. Put on clean towel to cool and become crisp. Will keep indefinitely if stored in a dry place. Before serving, dip each sheet of *Haringkake* in cold water, drain, and wrap in towel or wax paper to soften. Spread sheets with butter and any variety of assorted toppings; sugar, jams, cheeses, cold meats or peanut butter. Roll up and cut to size as desired.

West Coast Lefse
Kraatekake

Olive Nordby of Madison, Wis., writes: "This was Dr. (Eugene) Nordby's mother's recipe (Lucile Korsrud Nordby). We all liked Kraatekake *better than lefse. I would help her, as it's easiest with two working, taking turns rolling and frying. Even then, the dough fights back and it's difficult." All four of his grandparents came from Norway in the 1860s to the Decorah, Ia., and Lee, Ill., areas.*

2 pkgs. yeast
4 cups milk
¹/₂ cup butter
¹/₂ cup sugar
12 to 14 cups flour

Mix as for bread; dough should be a little firmer than bread. Let rise.

Knead down; let rise again until light. Divide into good-sized biscuits and cover with damp cloth to keep from drying out. Roll each one out on floured cloth with grooved rolling pin until thin, as for lefse. This is difficult as dough springs back. Use sharp pointed rolling pin to mark. Bake on hot greased griddle, turning as one side browns. Spread out cakes until cool and crisp. Makes about 50.

To serve, place between dampened dish towels until softened to consistency of lefse. Spread with butter and sugar as you would lefse.

"I make half a recipe, about twenty-eight cakes. These can be stored in covered containers or plastic sacks indefinitely when dry."

Oatmeal Flatbread
Havremel flatbrød

Norma Anderson Wangsness of Decorah, Ia., is a rosemaler and a photographic craftsman.

$^1/_2$ **cup sugar**
$^3/_4$ **cup melted butter**
$^1/_2$ **tsp. salt**
1$^1/_2$ **cups buttermilk**
1 **tsp. soda**

3 **cups white flour (or 2 cups white and 1 cup whole wheat)**
2 **cups quick-cooking oats**

Cream together sugar and melted butter. Add salt. Add soda to buttermilk and then add to the creamed mixture alternately with the flour. Add the oats.

Divide mixture into two log shapes. Divide, as you work, into $^1/_3$-cup portions and shape each into a round ball. Press down and roll on pastry cloth with a rolling pin covered with pastry sleeve. Roll until paper-thin. Use a lefse stick and roll the dough on stick; lift and unroll on cookie sheet.

Either cut with pastry cutter into squares before baking or bake and then break into pieces. Bake at 350 degrees F until lightly browned, about 8 minutes. Remove and stack. Store in covered container.

"We like to spread it with butter. You may use pickled herring with it or *gjetost* (goat cheese). It can also be served on an hors d'oeuvre tray."

Mother's Dark Rye Bread
Mors rugbrød

Florence Shjeflo Buck of Tacoma, Washington, is a member of the board of the Norwegian-American Museum in Decorah, Ia., and a member of the Collegium and Scandinavian Cultural Council at Pacific Lutheran University. She teaches rosemaling and was co-founder of the Western Rosemalers Association, of which she is a past president. Her father came from Trondheim and her mother's family from Østfold.

"This bread was always baked by my mother, Judith Nellie Rudd Shjeflo of North Dakota, when any of the children returned home after a lengthy absence. The aroma of fresh homemade bread, butter, and her special homemade jam served with coffee was the sweetest welcome we ever wanted."

Immigrant Ship

2 Tbsp. sugar
1 cup warm water
2 pkg. dry yeast
2 cups white flour
1 1/2 cups dark rye flour
1 tsp. salt
1/2 cup plus 1 Tbsp. molasses
1 1/4 cups hot water
2 Tbsp. melted shortening
4 cups white flour, approximately

In small mixing bowl add sugar to warm water. Dissolve. Sprinkle yeast over water. Set aside.

Put 2 cups white flour and the dark rye flour in large mixing bowl. Add salt and mix. Add molasses thinned with hot water. Add melted shortening. Mix. Add yeast. Mix. Gradually add remaining flour.

Flour bread board and knead dough 8 to 10 minutes, until elastic. Put dough in greased bowl and let rise until double in bulk.

Punch down and knead lightly. Divide into three equal portions. Shape into loaves and place in three individual 9"x 5" greased glass loaf pans. Let rise.

When double in size, bake in preheated oven at 375 degrees F for approximately 50 minutes.

—117

Whole-Wheat Bread
Hvetebrød

Dagny A. Schiotz of Minneapolis was the daughter of the Rev. A.O. Aasen, who emigrated from Norway and was a pastor of the Lutheran church until his death at 100 years of age. Her husband, the Rev. Fredrik A. Schiotz, has an illustrious background in the Lutheran church. He has served as president of the American Lutheran church and of the Lutheran World Federation of 70 million members. He is on the board of directors of the Norwegian-American Museum in Decorah, Ia. His autobiography, One Man's Story, *was published by the Augsburg Publishing House. The Rev. Mr. Schiotz says of this recipe: "There has been one item in her baking that I have especially enjoyed. I refer to her whole wheat bread. Many people have tasted it and given it solid approval."*

1 tsp. sugar
3 pkgs. dry yeast
$^1/_2$ cup lukewarm potato water
1 Tbsp. apple cider vinegar
1$^3/_4$ cups warm milk
$^1/_2$ cup oil (sunflower or sesame, if you wish)
$^1/_2$ cup dark molasses
$^1/_2$ cup brown sugar, firmly packed
$^1/_2$ cup rolled oats
1 egg, beaten
1 Tbsp. honey
1 cup whole wheat flour (or $^1/_2$ cup soy flour and $^1/_2$ cup rice flour)
1 cup rye flour
5 cups white flour
1 tsp. salt
sesame seed

Dissolve sugar and yeast in potato water. Set aside. In large bowl, combine vinegar (to retard mold), milk, oil, molasses, brown sugar and oats. Stir thoroughly. Add yeast mixture, beaten egg, and honey. Add flours and salt and beat vigorously until smooth.

Turn out on floured board. Add more flour as needed. Knead until elastic, about $^1/_2$ hour. Put into greased bowl; turn once or twice. Cover. Wrap bowl in plastic bag. Let rise until double.

Divide into three parts. Shape into loaves. Dip loaves into milk, then into sesame seed. Place in greased pans, cover, and let rise until double in size. Bake at 350 degrees F about 45 to 50 minutes. To test, tap crust for hollow sound. Remove from pans and cover to cool.

This decoration on butter molds was made by carving designs in reverse to stand out in relief on the molded butter. In this 1801 mold, the Lion of Norway and the crest of the king of Denmark are at right. Vesterheim collection.

Christmas Bread
Julekake

Barbara Hanson Bulman, Forest City, Ia. "Both of my grandfathers were John Hansons from Norway. My brother John K. Hanson carries on the family name. All four of my grandparents came from Norway via sailship after long, difficult journeys."

- $^1/_2$ **cup butter or margarine**
- **2 cups sugar**
- **3 eggs**
- **5 cups flour**
- **2 tsp. baking powder**
- **2 cups heavy sour cream**
- **1 tsp. soda dissolved in small amount of warm water**
- **1 tsp. ground cardamom**

Cream butter or margarine and sugar. Add eggs. Add sifted dry ingredients with sour cream and soda.

Divide dough in three parts and put in bread loaf pans. Bake for 45 minutes at 350 degrees F, or until it pulls away from sides of pans. Cakes should be golden.

While still hot, slice quickly and carefully as you would bread. It is rich and crumbles easily. Place slices on cookie sheets and toast in oven until lightly browned and dry, but not too brown.

After it is cooled, store in flat container to keep from crumbling, as it is dry.

"Our family wants it especially for holidays and visits home. You have to taste it to love it. Such a fun one to dunk!"

Coffee Braid
Kaffe kranz

Sylvia Rusley Simonson of Minneapolis writes: "For thirty-one years, I was a pastor's wife and for four years the wife of the U.S. ambassador to Ethiopia, so entertaining was a necessity."

2 cups milk, scalded
1 cup butter
2 pkgs. dry yeast
¹/₄ cup lukewarm water
1 tsp. sugar
5 eggs, well-beaten
1¹/₄ cups sugar
1 tsp. vanilla
1 to 2 tsp. cardamom
7³/₄ cups unbleached flour
Frosting:
1 egg, beaten
¹/₂ cup butter
1 pound powdered sugar
¹/₂ tsp. vanilla
¹/₂ tsp. almond flavoring
chopped nuts for topping

Scald milk, add butter, and let cool until lukewarm. Dissolve yeast in lukewarm water with 1 teaspoon sugar. Beat eggs well; add 1¹/₄ cups sugar and beat. Pound cardamom in a pestle until fine. Add vanilla and cardamom to mixture. Add flour and beat well. Let rise until double in bulk.

Put on floured board, adding more flour (as little as possible) before dividing into three parts.

Roll out one at a time in rectangular shape, about 10"x4." Cut lengthwise into six strips, braiding by threes to make six braids in all. Put two braids on each cookie sheet. Let rise about 2 hours in cold oven out of drafts.

After removing dough, preheat oven to 350 degrees F. Bake 15 minutes. When cool, frost with frosting made by beating egg with butter, powdered sugar, and flavorings. Sprinkle nuts on top.

Hardtack

Dagney Johansen is a student at the Scandinavian Language Institute. We received her recipe from Issa Parker of the Nordic Heritage Museum in Seattle, Wash. Former Director Marion Nelson of Vesterheim says the Norwegian breakfast often includes hardtack, a rye bread and a thin crisp flatbrød.

2 cups white flour
2 cups graham flour
¹/₂ cup white sugar
1 tsp. soda
¹/₂ tsp. salt
1 Tbsp. anise seed
¹/₂ cup shortening
1¹/₂ cups buttermilk

Mix dry ingredients. Cut in shortening. Add buttermilk. Roll out thinly. Cut into diamond-shaped pieces. Place on a greased cookie sheet. Bake at 400 degrees F for 12 to 15 minutes.

Norwegian Christmas Bread
Julekake

Eunice C. Stoen of Decorah has published her own cookbook called Euny's Cookbook. *She and her husband, Wilbur, live on a dairy and hog farm in northeast Iowa.*

2 pkgs. dry yeast
¹/₂ cup warm water
1 tsp. sugar
1 cup milk, scalded
¹/₂ cup butter
1 egg, beaten
¹/₂ cup sugar
¹/₂ tsp. salt
³/₄ tsp. cardamom
5 cups flour, approximately
¹/₂ cup citron
¹/₂ cup candied cherries
¹/₂ cup white raisins

Dissolve yeast in warm water and a little sugar. Scald milk and add butter; cool to lukewarm. Add egg and then yeast mixture. Add sugar, salt, and cardamom. Beat in 2 cups flour and mix well. Mix fruit with a little of the remaining flour so it doesn't stick together and add. Stir in rest of flour. Knead on floured cloth until smooth. Place in greased bowl. Cover and let rise until doubled. Divide into two parts and form round loaves. Put on greased cookie sheets or pie pans. Let rise until nearly double.

Bake at 350 degrees F for 30 to 40 minutes. While warm, brush with soft butter or decorate with powdered sugar icing mixed with almond flavoring, then almonds and more candied cherries.

"This is a Christmas bread, but I use it other times, too. Slice a round loaf, cut slices in half on an angle or in smaller pieces, butter, and serve as fancy sandwiches. This is delicious toasted, buttered, and served with tea. It makes a pretty gift, wrapped in foil with a big red bow on top."

Buttercup
This little boy ate so much of his mother's baking he was known as Buttercup in Norwegian folklore. His dog was named Goldtooth. Illustration by Theodor Kittelsen.

Christmas Bread
Julebrød

Martha Torrison of Schaumburg, Ill. "My grandparents came from Norway. After several moves they ended up in Manitowoc, Wis., ... My father, one of 12, became a doctor."

2 cups milk, scalded
1 or 2 cakes yeast
¹/₄ cup warm water and
  1 Tbsp. sugar
1 cup sugar
7 to 8 cups flour
¹/₂ cup butter
1 cup raisins
1 cup cut-up citron
2 tsp. cardamom
¹/₂ cup blanched almonds
2 tsp. salt

Scald milk and cool to lukewarm. Dissolve yeast in the warm water and 1 Tbsp. sugar. To the milk add sugar, yeast, and half of the flour. Beat thoroughly. Add butter, fruit, cardamom, nuts, salt, and enough flour to make a stiff dough. Knead, cover and let rise until double.

Form two loaves. Let rise. When double in bulk, bake at 350 degrees F about 1 hour.

Bishop's Bread
Brød

Ruth Wickney, Northwood, N.D., says this recipe is "elegant for the holidays and especially for those who do not like fruitcake. It freezes well. This was Mrs. J. A. Aasgard's recipe. Dr. Aasgard was the presiding bishop of the Norwegian Lutheran Church before the days of current mergers."

1 cup sugar
3 eggs
1¹/₂ cups flour
1¹/₂ tsp. baking powder
1 cup whole walnuts
1 cup whole Brazil nuts
1 cup whole maraschino
  cherries
1 cup whole pitted dates
1 8-oz. bar semi-sweet or
  sweet chocolate, cut in
  large chunks

Mix sugar and eggs well. Add flour and baking powder. Mix well. Add whole nuts, cherries, dates, and chocolate. Hand mix. Prepare loaf pan by lining with heavy waxed paper. Pour batter into lined pan. Cover pan loosely with excess waxed paper. Bake at 325 degrees F 1 hour and 25 minutes. Fold back the waxed paper when batter has risen (about 50 to 60 minutes after it has been in oven).

Oatmeal Crackers
Havrekjeks

Jackie Bjoin of Golden Valley, Minn., first tasted these crackers at Skogfjorden, the Norwegian Language Camp, and then made them to serve to the kick-off committee for the Nordic Brunch in Minneapolis. They are delicious and easy to make.

1 cup cornflakes
1 cup bran flakes
2 cups rolled oats
2 cups flour
$^1/_2$ cup sugar
1 cup margarine
1 tsp. soda
$^1/_2$ cup hot water

Measure cornflakes and bran flakes and then crush. Add oats, flour, and sugar. Cut in margarine with pastry blender. Add soda which has been dissolved in hot water. Blend well. Divide dough into four equal parts. With a sleeve-covered lefse rolling pin, roll out each part separately to $^1/_{16}$-inch thickness on a floured pastry cloth. With a pizza or *fattigmann* cutter, cut into 2"x3" rectangles. Place on an ungreased cookie sheet. Bake for 8 to 10 minutes at 350 degrees F. Cool. Crackers are tender, so store carefully.

Rusks
Kavring

Thora Leonard of Story City, Iowa: "I have had the good fortune to visit the Scandinavian countries. From pleasant memories of my visit I say, 'Jeg kan ikke glemme gamle Norge!'"

$^1/_2$ cup margarine
$^1/_3$ cup sugar
1 cup white flour
1 cup whole-wheat or rye flour
1 tsp. soda
2 tsp. baking powder
$^1/_2$ tsp. cream of tartar
$^3/_4$ cup buttermilk

Cream together margarine and sugar. Sift together other dry ingredients. Add to creamed mixture alternately with buttermilk. Roll flat with rolling pin to $^1/_4$-inch thickness on lightly floured pastry board. Cut 2-inch rounds. Place on ungreased baking sheet and bake at 400 degrees F until light brown.

Split each biscuit in half. Place on baking sheet and bake at 200 degrees about 5 minutes or until light brown. Makes about 4 dozen. Can be frozen. "These *kavrings* are made especially for Christmas festivities in Norwegian homes. We always serve them for breakfast Christmas Day."

Blitz Torte

Marlys Lien of Calmar, Iowa, received this recipe from her mother-in-law, Grace Lien. Grace's mother, Cecilia Borness, also enjoyed this cake. "Engvold Borness, Cecilia's husband, came to America in 1902 at the age of 21. He began working on farms, earning about $25 a month in the summer. In the winter he worked in lumber camps. So many grandchildren and great-grandchildren loved him and enjoyed his tales of coming to America. I feel so fortunate to have known Engvold and Cecilia."

> 4 egg yolks
> $^1/_2$ cup butter
> $^1/_2$ cup sugar
> scant 1 cup flour
> 5 Tbsp. milk
> 1 tsp. vanilla
> dash salt
> 1$^1/_2$ tsp. baking powder

Meringue:
> 4 egg whites
> $^3/_4$ cup sugar
> nuts

Filling:
> pudding or whipped cream

Beat egg yolks, butter, and sugar. Add flour, milk, vanilla, salt, and baking powder. Beat well. Put in two layer pans, which have been greased and lined with foil. Beat four egg whites until stiff. Add $^3/_4$ cup sugar slowly, mixing well. Spread this meringue mixture on cakes before baking. Sprinkle with nuts. Bake at 350 degrees F for 20 minutes. Lift out onto wax paper to cool. Place one cake on serving plate, meringue side down. Put filling of pudding or whipped cream on top of meringue. Place other layer on top, meringue side up.

"This has been the most asked for birthday cake in our family for many years. It has become a birthday tradition."

Great-grandmother's Gingerbread
Oldemors pepperbrød

Norma Wangsness of Decorah sends this recipe, which was a favorite of her mother, Christina Lotvedt Anderson. "She lived to be 90," writes Norma, *"and she started the embroidery of my costume* (bunad) *when she was 80, finishing when she was 85. She did better embroidery at 80 than she did at 60. "This recipe is over 100 years old. It was the recipe of Aasta Kaasa Lotvedt, my grandmother, who came from Heddal, Telemark.*

$^1/_2$ **cup sugar**
$^1/_2$ **cup butter and lard, mixed**
1 **egg, beaten**
1 **cup molasses**
$2^1/_2$ **cups sifted flour**
$1^1/_2$ **tsp. soda**
1 **tsp. cinnamon**
1 **tsp. ginger**
$^1/_2$ **tsp. cloves**
$^1/_2$ **tsp. salt**
1 **cup hot water**

Cream sugar and shortening. Add beaten egg and molasses. Add dry ingredients that have been sifted together. Add hot water last and beat until smooth. Bake in greased, shallow pan at 350 degrees F about 45 to 50 minutes. Makes 15 portions.

This kubbestol, *including the view on the opposite page, is in the Vesterheim collection. It is a superb example of acanthus carving by Halvor Lie, of Kristiansand, Norway, in the early 1900s. A* kubbestol *is made from one section of wood. Some are plain without carving and others may have rosemaling.*

Vesterheim photos

Cakes and Cookies

The Princess

Princess Sonja, now Her Majesty Queen of Norway, was a special guest at a Vesterheim celebration at the Minneapolis Institute of Art Nov. 4, 1979. Women of the Nornen Lodge #41, Madison, Minnesota, baked the cookies that were served.

When Norwegian cooks serve coffee after dinner, seven is considered the magic number for the variety of cookies to accompany it. The seven selected by the Madison women were fattigmann, krumkaker, rosettes, Berlinerkranser, sandbakkels, spritz, *and* goro.

Prince's Cake
Fyrstekake

Sigurd Daasvand of Brooklyn, N.Y., is former editor-in-chief of the Norwegian language newspaper Nordisk Tidende, *published every Thursday in Brooklyn. He was decorated by King Olav V of Norway with the St. Olav's Medal and by* Nordmann-Forbundet (Norseman Federation) in Oslo.

1 1/2 **cups flour**
1 **tsp. baking powder**
1/2 **cup sugar**
1/2 **cup plus 1 Tbsp. butter**
1 **egg or 2 egg yolks**
Almond filling:
1 **cup ground almonds**
1 **cup powdered sugar**
2 **egg whites, slightly beaten**

Mix dry ingredients into mixing bowl. Blend in butter with pastry blender or with your fingertips until mixture resembles coarse flour. Thoroughly beat in egg or egg yolks. Chill well. If you wish blanched almonds, scald them. Unblanched give a better flavor. Grind almonds once, then grind a second time with powdered sugar. Blend thoroughly with beaten egg whites until mixture is firm and smooth. Chill.

Press 2/3 of the chilled dough into an 8-inch round ungreased cake pan, covering bottom and sides. Spread almond mixture evenly over dough. Roll remainder of dough out to 1/8-inch thickness and cut into eight strips 1/2-inch in width. Lay four of the strips parallel to each other across top of filling. Arrange remaining four strips at right angles, weaving to form a lattice pattern. Cut out another 1/2-inch-wide strip and press around edge of cake. Brush with slightly beaten egg. Bake at 375 degrees F for 25 to 30 minutes or until golden brown and thoroughly baked. Leave cake on rack a few minutes before carefully loosening sides and removing from pan. Cut into wedges.

"This is good to serve . . . with a nice cup of coffee and also at birthday parties. Our family is very fond of this cake. In fact, we grew up with it back home in Norway, where mother used to bake it."

Else's Whipped Cream Layer Cake
Else's Bløtkake

Else Sevig, Minneapolis, and her husband, Mike, are Norwegian folk singers who have recorded several albums. They own Skandisk Inc., a publisher and distributor.

> **6 large eggs**
> **³/₄ cup sugar**
> **1 cup flour**
> **Filling:**
> **6 to 9 Tbsp. milk**
> **4 cups whipping cream**
> **1 Tbsp. powdered sugar**
> **¹/₂ tsp. vanilla**
> **1 to 2 cups berries or fruit (strawberries, pineapple, peaches, or apricots), fresh or frozen, or 1 cup finely chopped walnuts**

Beat eggs and sugar until stiff, about 10 minutes at high speed with electric mixer. Gently fold in sifted flour. Pour into 10- to 12-inch springform pan, the bottom greased and floured. If you use another type of pan, line bottom with waxed paper. Bake in center of oven at 350 degrees F about 30 minutes or until a toothpick inserted in center comes out clean. Leave oven door open 2 minutes before taking cake out of oven. When completely cool, remove cake from pan.

Cut cake in two or three layers, using a long, thin knife. Rotate the cake as you cut. Sprinkle 3 tablespoons milk over each layer. Whip the cream with powdered sugar and vanilla. Mix fruit, berries, or nuts with two-thirds of the whipped cream mixture and spread between layers. Put remaining whipped cream on top and sides and use for decorating. Extra berries and fruit can also be added for decoration.

Cake can be filled the day before serving, in which case use less milk on each layer. Cover and store in cool place. This cake is used for Norwegian birthday parties, weddings, or any festive occasion.

Whipped Cream Layer Cake
Norwegian Bløtkake

Lottie Huse Brown sends this recipe from Clifton, Texas, where there is a large Norwegian-American population. "When we visited Norway, this cake was served in practically every home. It is full of calories and very delicious."

4 cups flour
1 cup butter
2 tsp. baking powder
3 eggs
1 cup sugar
vanilla pudding
prepared whipped topping
jam, strawberries, sliced
    peaches, banana, or
    pinapple chunks

Mix flour, butter, and baking powder. In another bowl beat eggs; add sugar. Combine two mixtures and mix well. Knead. Divide into nine sections and roll each to plate size. Bake on greased cookie sheet at 350 degrees F 10 to 15 minutes, or until lightly browned. Use three layers for each cake. Put pudding and fruit between layers and cover with whipped topping. Decorate with fruit, nuts, coconut, etc.

Le Ann Wangsness-Bahr of Maple Grove, Minn., said after a trip abroad, "In Norway, Bløtkake is served at the table, where each piece is cut and placed on the plate. If the cake remains standing and you are single, you are soon to be married. A 10-year-old friend always tipped her piece over with her fork."

Raspberry Cake
Bringebærkake

Marilyn Wang Engwall, Rochester, Minn. Her husband, Clarence W. Engwall, is a board member of Vesterheim. She says, "My Norsk grandmother came from Innset, Østerdal, and my Norsk grandfather from Os, Østerdal. I have visited both family farms, still owned by our relatives. Both farm homes still contain all the antique furniture and artifacts. Each family farm also has a sæter (mountain farm). My husband and I have been to Norway six times. This cake is typical of what is served there."

$1^1/_2$ cups flour
$^1/_2$ cup sugar
1 tsp. baking powder
$^1/_2$ cup butter
1 egg
$^1/_2$ cup raspberry jam, divided

Filling:
$^1/_2$ cup butter
$^2/_3$ cup sugar
$^1/_2$ tsp. almond extract
2 eggs
1 cup finely ground
    blanched almonds (like
    coarse corn meal)

Frosting:
$^1/_2$ cup powdered sugar
2 tsp. lemon juice

Grease a 9"x1¹/₂" springform pan. Blend flour, sugar, and baking powder. Add butter and mix as for pie crust. Add egg and blend with a fork until flour is moistened. Press dough evenly on bottom of pan. Spread ¹/₄ cup raspberry jam over dough. Cover and chill while making filling.

For filling: Cream butter and sugar. Add extract. Add eggs one at a time, beating well. Mix in ground almonds. Spoon filling on top of jam. Bake at 350 degrees for 50 minutes. Cool in pan and remove cake carefully. Spread remaining ¹/₄ cup jam over top. Mix powdered sugar and lemon juice together and drizzle on top of jam.

Can be made ahead of time and frozen.

Apple Cake
Eplekake

Mrs. Lawrence O. Hauge of Edina, Minn., writes: "My mother and father, both Norwegian immigrants, met in Minneapolis. Our home life was very Norwegian-oriented, for which I have been thankful."

2 eggs, well-beaten
1¹/₂ cups sugar, half brown and half white
2 tsp. vanilla
1¹/₂ cups flour
2 tsp. baking powder

¹/₄ **tsp. salt**
2¹/₂ **cups diced apples**
¹/₂ **cup coarsely broken nutmeats**

Beat eggs, sugar, and vanilla together. Sift dry ingredients together and add to other mixture. Add apples and nuts. Bake in a 13"x9" pan at 375 degrees F for 30 to 35 minutes. Serve cold with whipped cream.

Mother's Sour Cream Frosting
Mors rømmekrem

Ruth Wickney of Northwood, N.D., writes: "This frosting on white or Lady Baltimore cake was made every other Saturday throughout my growing-up years. It was special and is remembered with nostalgia. (Alternate Saturdays it was chocolate cake!)"

4 eggs or 5 yolks and 1 egg
1 cup sugar
1 cup sour cream
1 tsp. almond extract
chopped nuts

Put eggs or yolks and one whole egg, sugar, and sour cream in double boiler. Stir and cook until thick. Remove from burner and add almond extract. Frost cooled cake. Sprinkle with chopped nuts.

Norwegian Wedding Cake
Kransekake

Kransekake, or ring (tree) cake, is a festival tradition in Norway. It is served at Christmas because of its tree shape, at weddings because of its impressive height, and for anniversaries and birthdays because of its many layers. It can be made in as many rings as there are years to observe.

It can be served as a bridegroom's cake at wedding receptions, where each guest is given a small piece in addition to the regular cake.

The cake is so decorative that some people use it as a centerpiece and bake extra rings for serving. The cake tower is hollow, so a bottle of wine can be hidden inside as an extra treat after the cake is eaten.

Although the recipe for *kransekake* is simple, you may want to bake a few practice rings before you attempt the "real thing." Try half a recipe to learn the cutting and baking techniques.

Here are two versions of *kransekake* from Decorah, Iowa, cooks. The first has a light delicate flavor and a chewy, cookie-like texture. It is baked in eighteen concentric ring mold pans. These pans are available at Scandinavian specialty shops. Local bakeries can usually provide the almond paste.

The second recipe is made of a rich cookie dough with the taste of a butter or *spritz* cookie. It is baked on twenty-six squares of aluminum-wrapped cardboard. This is the answer for those who do not want to invest in the ring mold pans.

Both recipes produce baked rings that are stacked to make this conical cake with a hollow center. To serve, simply lift off each layer and break into serving-size pieces.

Arla Erickson Lyon's Kransekake

1 lb. almond paste
1 lb. powdered sugar, sifted
2 egg whites, unbeaten
$1/4$ cup powdered sugar for kneading

Mix almond paste and powdered sugar. Add egg whites. Mix well. Place bowl in hot water and knead dough until it is lukewarm. Turn out on board sprinkled with $1/4$ cup powdered sugar. Let rest 10 minutes.

Knead 2 to 3 minutes. Press dough through cookie press into greased ring forms. Bake at 300 degrees F for 20 minutes. Do not remove rings from forms until cold. Place rings on top of one another, icing each one with frosting as you stack them.

Frosting:
1¹/₂ cups powdered sugar, sifted
1 egg white, unbeaten
1 tsp. vinegar

Mix well and drizzle over cake rings. Arla sometimes stacks five or six rings and freezes them. Later she stacks the rest of them to complete the cake. The rings freeze well.

She says, "My husband used an electric drill to remove the points of the star on my cookie press so this enables me to press dough out faster. Or, you can roll out by hand and lay in the pans. But if you are making seven pounds at a time, you try to find the easiest way."

If you do not wish to make the recipe into rings, you can cut into rectangles for cookies and frost them.

Norma Wangsness's Kransekake

2 cups soft butter
1 cup almond paste
2 cups sifted powdered sugar
2 tsp. almond extract
4 egg yolks
5 cups sifted flour

It will take 1¹/₂ recipes to make the total twenty-six-ring cake.

Cream together until smooth the butter, almond paste, powdered sugar, and almond extract. Beat egg yolks in well. Measure flour after it has been sifted and add gradually, mixing until very smooth.

Place paper patterns on lightly greased cookie sheets. Put dough into cookie press or pastry bag. Press out to shape rings around *inside* edges of paper patterns. Chill 15 minutes if desired.

Bake in oven at 350 degrees for 15 minutes or until very lightly browned. Cool on paper pattern.

To assemble cake, drizzle some frosting on platter. This will anchor cake. Place largest ring on frosting. Apply frosting in scallops on first ring. Place next largest ring on top and decorate and stack in order until you have used all twenty-six layers. The scalloped frosting will hold each ring in place.

Frosting:
  1 ¹/₂ cups sifted powdered sugar
  1 egg white
  1 tsp. vinegar

Stir together. If not stiff enough, add more powdered sugar. Put in pastry tube with small round tip.

To decorate, use small Norwegian flags on stick pins and insert in cake. Or buy marzipan fruits and stick on toothpicks. Slide toothpicks between layers to hold in place. Or wrap tiny presents or notes and decorate for a birthday party.

To serve, break into 2¹/₂-inch pieces. Makes about 60 to 75 broken pieces.

"For each of my daughters' weddings, I made five of these. Two of the five were used as centerpieces with one behind to use for the actual serving. We used Norwegian flags to decorate and placed the cakes on Norwegian blue plates with fresh ivy and baby's breath around the base."

Evonne Anderson of Moorhead, Minn., says, "In Norway this is also used for confirmations and graduations."

Cardboard Paper Patterns

You will need to cut twenty-six squares of cardboard. The first will be a 2-inch square, the second a 2¹/₄-inch square, etc., each one ¹/₄-inch larger than the one before. The twenty-sixth layer square will be 8¹/₄ inches square. Cover each square with heavy duty aluminum wrap, covering completely to prevent scorching.

Using a compass, make a circle 1 inch in diameter on the #1 square, on number two a 1¹/₄-inch circle, etc., until number twenty-six, which will be 7¹/₄-inches in diameter. Number each pattern to keep them in order.

Drop Cookies
Gudbrandsdalkaker

Rolf H. Erickson of Evanston, Ill., is on the board of directors of the Norwegian-American Museum and the Norwegian-American Historical Association.

He writes: "My mother's Aunt Berit Ramseth Jacobson introduced me to the Gudbrandsdal cookie thirty-three years ago. As a child of eight, I stuffed myself with them on a Christmas visit to her home in Milwaukee.

"Highly pleased that I liked her baking, she filled my pockets for the

trip home, admonishing me to remember that the Gudbrandsdal cookie was her mother's recipe and had been made and served at their home in Tynset, Østerdal.

"As an adult I learned that Great-grandmother Barbro, unable to afford almonds after her arrival in Wisconsin in 1888, substituted hickory nuts—free for the gathering from farm woodlots.

"In 1970, Borghild Ramseth Nissen found in an old family cookbook that almonds were the original ingredient. So the genuine Gudbrandsdal again appears on Ramseth Christmas tables."

1 cup sugar
1 cup vegetable shortening, butter, or margarine
1 cup cornstarch
2 cups flour
1 cup whipping cream
few drops almond flavoring
1 cup sliced almonds

Blend sugar and shortening. Add rest of ingredients in order, blending after each addition. This is a drop cookie and should not be larger than a half-dollar.

Bake in slow oven at 250 degrees F until cookie is light golden brown around edges and white in center.

Butter Rings
Berlinerkranser

Eleanor Anundsen of Decorah, Ia., sent this recipe, which was handed down from her husband's grandmother, Helma Anundsen. Helma's husband, B. Anundsen, was founder (1874) and publisher of the Norwegian newspaper Decorah-Posten. *In the 1920s, the* Decorah-Posten *had a circulation of 45,000. It was consolidated in 1972 with* Western Viking *of Seattle, Wash.*

3 hard-boiled egg yolks
4 raw egg yolks
1 cup plus 2 Tbsp. sugar
5 to 5¹/₂ cups flour
1 pound butter
1 egg white

Mash yolks of hard-boiled eggs. Add yolks of raw eggs, blending into a smooth paste. Add sugar, beating well. Add flour and butter alternately, using your hands. Roll pieces of dough to the thickness of a pencil, about 3 inches long. Shape each like a bow. Whip egg white and brush on top of each cookie. Bake at 350 degrees F until light golden brown. Makes about seven dozen cookies.

"We still use this recipe at Christmas time. They should be stored in a cool place. They also freeze well."

Pretzel

In Norway, the baker's sign is a large pretzel.

Poor Man's Cakes
Fattigmann

Helen M. Haatvedt of Decorah says: "My grandmother and my mother, both of whom were experts at making this cookie, insisted that it be handled very carefully and not allowed to be fried too dark or not browned enough. The cookies had to be uniform in size and thickness and could not be tough from too much stirring. This recipe goes back to 1882."

> 1 whole egg
> 3 egg yolks
> 4 Tbsp. cream
> 4 tsp. sugar
> 1 Tbsp. melted butter
> $1/4$ tsp. ground cardamom
> $1^1/2$ cups flour, approximately

Beat egg and egg yolks slightly. Add other ingredients. Use enough flour to make a soft dough. Mix, handling as little and as lightly as possible. Roll out on floured cloth and cut in 2"x2" diamond shapes. Fry in hot lard until very lightly browned. Drain on brown paper and dust with more powdered sugar when cool.

Kringle

Marilyn Haugen Istad of Decorah, Iowa, says: "This is the recipe used by my daughter Jan and her teenage friends about thirteen years ago to make kringles. As a demonstration in a store window for the Nordic Fest, they rolled and baked these tasty goodies and sold them to the visitors."

> $5^1/4$ cups flour
> 2 tsp. baking powder
> pinch salt
> $2/3$ cup margarine
> 2 cups sugar
> 1 tsp. vanilla
> 2 egg yolks, unbeaten
> 2 tsp. soda
> 2 cups buttermilk

Mix flour, baking powder and salt and set aside. Cream margarine, sugar, and vanilla. Add egg yolks. Add soda to buttermilk and add to creamed mixture before foaming stops. Add dry ingredients. Chill at least 3 hours.

Place a clean dish towel on flat surface. Flour well. Drop a teaspoonful of dough onto floured towel. Roll into a long rope, about 6 inches long and $3/8$ inch in diameter. Place on greased cookie sheets, making figure 8s or pretzel design with the dough rope.

Bake 4 minutes on bottom shelf

of oven; move to top shelf and bake 2 minutes longer until lightly browned on bottom.

Anise Kringle

Dagney Johansen gave this traditional Norwegian cookie recipe to the Nordic Heritage Museum of Seattle, whose director is Marianne Forssblad. The museum, small and growing, represents Scandinavian heritage. Honorary trustees include the consuls of Norway, Sweden, Finland, Iceland, and Denmark.

> 1^1/$_2$ **cups granulated sugar**
> 1 **cup butter or shortening**
> 1 **whole egg**
> 4 **egg yolks**
> ^{1}/$_2$ **tsp. baking powder**
> 2 **heaping tsp. anise seed**
> 3 **cups white flour**

Mix all ingredients, in order given, in one bowl. Roll small amounts of dough to pencil thickness. Cut into 8- or 9-inch lengths. Form into pretzel shapes. Arrange on a greased cookie sheet and bake at 350 degrees F until light brown. Makes about four dozen.

Rosettes

Lloyd George Melgard of Warren, Minn., describes himself as a retired farmer, world traveler, correspondent, happy bachelor, and a collector of cookbooks, interested in fine antiques and porcelains. He has published a history of his community. "My father's three uncles and an aunt came to Black River Falls, Wis., from the Melgard Farm in Sør Fron above Hundorp in Gudbrandsdal around the time of the Civil War."

> 2 **eggs**
> 1 **tsp. sugar**
> ^{1}/$_4$ **tsp. salt**
> 1 **cup milk**
> 1 **cup flour**

Beat eggs slightly with sugar and salt. Add milk and flour and beat until smooth. Heat *rosette* iron in hot lard or vegetable shortening to 370 degrees F. For the first *rosette*, wipe excess fat from iron with paper towels and dip into batter, but do not allow to come over top of iron. Return iron to hot fat and immerse. Fry for about 20 seconds or until color desired.

In removing iron from fat, turn it over to drain. Jolt *rosette* off iron and repeat. If *rosette* falls off iron in hot fat, you do not have enough flour in batter. If *rosette* is thick, you have too much flour and need to thin a bit with milk.

This recipe makes 40 *rosettes.* When you are finished cooking *rosettes,* place them on paper towels on a cookie sheet with towels between each layer. Put in oven at 300 degrees F. Turn off heat. Allow to cool. This will remove excess fat from *rosettes* and improve them. They may be dusted with powdered sugar before serving. In Norway they are sometimes stacked three high with whipped cream between them and then topped with fruit.

"I have used this recipe for years with good results. I make it for giving to many families at Christmas time. My home reeks of Crisco after completing that project, and my feet hurt from standing and frying the *rosettes* one at a time."

Ethelyn Thompson of Hollandale, Wis.; Hazel Hove Hendrickson of Ossian, Iowa; and Bernice Oellien of Madison, Minn. also sent in recipes for *rosettes.* Ethelyn Thompson wrote: "During my years of guiding at Little Norway, I developed an interest in stave churches. It took me three trips to Norway to see all thirty-one of them."

Frycakes
American *"Smultringer"*

This recipe was sent in by Barbara Hanson Bulman, Forest City, Iowa, for her 96-year-old mother, Gina J. Hanson Hanson, Forest City, Iowa. Her son, John K. Hanson, is chairman of the board and chief executive officer of Winnebago Industries, Inc.

$1/3$ **cup shortening**
1 **cup sugar**
2 **eggs**
4 **cups flour**
4 **tsp. baking powder**
1 **cup milk**
$1/4$ **tsp. nutmeg**
pinch salt
$1/2$ **tsp. lemon extract**
oil for frying

Cream shortening and sugar; add eggs. Sift together dry ingredients and add alternately with milk to first mixture. Add flavoring. Mix well, but be careful not to overmix or to use too much flour. Chill dough for ease in rolling. Divide dough into two portions for rolling. Work on board with just enough flour to roll fairly thick. Cut with doughnut cutter and fry in hot oil at 370 degrees F. Turn cakes only once, when top shows cracks. Drain on paper towels.

Stryl
A type of krumkake

Ann Urness Gesme and her husband, Dean, of Cedar Rapids, Iowa, are "Norwegian all the way." All eight of her great-grandparents came from Norway, Sogning, on her father's side and Valdres on her mother's. Dean is secretary of Bygdelagenes Fellesraad, National Council of Bygdelags. In early twentieth-century America, Norwegian immigrants whose roots were in the same district in Norway organized into bygdelags. *Dean is president of Vestlandslaget with four different* bygdelags.

- ³/₄ **cup sugar**
- 1¹/₂ **cups flour**
- ¹/₂ **tsp. ground cardamom**
- 1 **cup whipping cream**
- ¹/₂ **cup half-and-half**
- ¹/₂ **cup milk**

Mix sugar, flour, and cardamom. Add whipping cream and stir in. Stir in half-and-half and then the milk. Bake on *krumkake* iron.

Increase the amount of half-and-half and decrease the amount of milk if a richer *krumkake* is desired. A bit of melted butter added will do the same thing. "The absence of butter and eggs makes this recipe unique. It's my favorite *krumkake* recipe.

Wafer Cones or Crumb Cake
Krumkake

Le Ann Wangsness-Bahr of Maple Grove, Minn. "The trick to eating krumkakes *is to insert the tip of your tongue in open center to bite off a piece. Otherwise, crumb cake!"*

- 3 **eggs, well-beaten**
- ¹/₂ **cup sugar**
- ¹/₂ **cup melted butter**
- ¹/₄ **tsp. salt**
- 1 **tsp. flavoring (almond and lemon extract)**
- ¹/₂ **cup flour**

Beat eggs well. Add sugar, melted butter, salt, and flavoring. Beat well. Stir in flour.

Heat *krumkake* iron on medium heat. Put a teaspoonful of batter on iron. Bake 1 minute or less, turn iron over, and bake until very lightly browned. Remove from iron and quickly roll on cone-shape form. Store in tight container.

Site to Remember

Near Coon Valley, Wisconsin, Norskedalen includes the Bekkum Homestead with eight pioneer log cabins and more.

Goro

Lillian Pederson of Marietta, Minn., sent this recipe for one variety of cookie served to Princess Sonja of Norway.

   3 eggs
   1 cup sugar
   1 cup sweet cream
   1 cup melted butter
2$^1/_2$ cups flour
   1 tsp. cinnamon or $^1/_4$ tsp. ground cardamom

Beat eggs well; add sugar and blend thoroughly. Add cream, melted butter, then sifted dry ingredients, and mix. Roll out thin and cut out, using paper pattern to fit a *goro* iron. Place on heated iron; turn to bake other side. After removing *goro,* cut in thirds while still warm. Store in air-tight container or a dry area.

Olive Nordby of Madison, Wis., uses cardamom in her *goro* cookies. She says: "The best cardamom comes in seed form, sold in bulk at herb or health food stores. Remove seeds from pods and crush with mortar and pestle. Since it is important to have the dough cold, it helps to have two people working, one taking sections from refrigerator and baking and the other cutting apart and stacking them."

Spiced Hermits

Marilyn Skaugstad of Iowa City, Iowa

   1 cup shortening
   2 cups sugar
   3 eggs
   1 tsp. cinnamon
   1 tsp. nutmeg
$^1/_2$ tsp. cloves
   2 tsp. lemon extract
   1 tsp. soda dissolved in
      1 Tbsp. hot water
   2 cups raisins, rinsed and ground
3$^1/_2$ cups all-purpose flour

Combine ingredients in order given and chill dough. Roll out thinly and cut with large round cookie cutter. Sprinkle with sugar and bake at 350 degrees F for 10 to 12 minutes. Makes a large batch.

Below: Christmas tree decoration, rosemaling by Norma Wangsness

Grandma Rosdail's Cookies
Oldemors kaker

This recipe comes from Rachel O. Southcombe of Newark, Ill., whose great-grandfather was Daniel Stenson Rosdail. He was one-sixth owner of the Restauration *and had the largest family on board, seven including the parents. "The woman the cookies are named after was the widow of John Rosdail, who came to America in 1825 on board the sloop* Restauration.*"*

- 1¹/₂ **cups raisins, boiled**
- 1 **cup butter or other shortening**
- 2 **cups sugar**
- 2 **eggs, beaten**
- 1 **cup, minus 2 Tbsp. sour milk**
- 1 **tsp. soda**
- 1 **tsp. vanilla**
- 2¹/₂ **to 3 cups flour**
- 1 **tsp. baking powder**

Boil raisins in just enough water to cover. Sweeten and cool. Drain.

Cream butter and sugar. Add beaten eggs. Add soda to sour milk and stir. Add sour milk and soda to first mixture. Add cooled raisins and vanilla. Add baking powder and enough flour to handle when rolling out.

Roll out on floured board and cut with cookie cutter. Place on greased cookie sheets. Bake at 350 to 375 degrees F until light brown.

Sandbakkels

Lois Wold Christenson of Decorah, Ia., a third-generation Norwegian whose family sings as the "Christenson Family Singers," sends this recipe. She and her husband, Paul, who is pastor of First Lutheran Church, have six children. They have performed on three Scandinavian and European tours and at the annual Nordic Fest.

- 2 **cups shortening (1 cup butter and 1 cup margarine)**
- 1 **cup sugar**
- 6 **Tbsp. whipping cream**
- 1 **Tbsp. brandy (or brandy flavoring)**
- 1 **egg**
- 6 **cups flour**

Cream shortening and sugar. Add cream, brandy, and egg. Slowly add flour until all is well-mixed. Chill slightly before pressing in tins.

Roll into small balls. Press into *sandbakkel* tins and keep pressing until thin layer covers bottom and sides. Trim off excess from edges.

Bake at 350 degrees F until light golden in color.

"You can purchase *sandbakkel* tins at Scandinavian shops. This recipe freezes well. It's delicious when filled with fruit, pie filling, etc., and topped with whipped cream, but also great plain."

Sandbakkels

Gyda Paulson-Thoen Mahlum of Beloit, Wis., won a gold medal in rosemaling in 1972 and has studied with teachers from Norway. Three examples of her rosemaling were in the traveling exhibit in Norway in 1975. Several pieces of her work have been purchased by the Norwegian-American Museum in Decorah, Ia. She is a member of the Valdres Samband and Hadeland Lag.

  $^1/_2$ **cup butter**
  $^1/_2$ **cup vegetable shortening**
  $^3/_4$ **cup sugar**
   1 **egg**
   1 **tsp. vanilla**
  $^1/_4$ **tsp. almond extract**
  2$^1/_4$ **cups flour**

Cream shortenings and sugar; add egg and flavorings and beat well. Sift flour and gradually add to creamed mixture. Mix well. Turn dough onto waxed paper and wrap. Chill in refrigerator for about 45 minutes. Preheat oven to 350 degrees F. Cut thin slices of dough and press into *sandbakkel* tins, beginning at the bottom and working upward to the top edge of the tin so it will not be too thick at the bottom. If dough becomes a little sticky, flour your fingers lightly.

Place on cookie sheet and bake for 15 minutes or until golden brown. Baking time may vary with the size of the tin. Cool in tins. When cool turn to release the *sandbakkels.* If necessary, tap the tin very gently. Makes 5 dozen.

Spritz

Irene O. Engebretson of Decorah, Ia.

   1 **cup butter or margarine**
  $^2/_3$ **cup sugar**
   3 **egg yolks**
   1 **tsp. almond extract**
  $^1/_2$ **tsp. vanilla**
  2$^1/_2$ **cups flour**

Cream shortening and sugar. Add egg yolks and extracts. Mix well. Add flour and mix well. Press dough onto cookie sheets through spritz cookie tube into different designs. Bake in oven at 350 degrees F until light golden brown.

Above: *Lingonberries*
Lingonberries grow in the Scandinavian countries and are similar to cranberries in the United States. They are used in jellies and can be used to marinate fish and meats.

Christmas Tarts

Dorothy Erickson Norby of Mabel, Minn., writes: "These cookies have always been served in my home starting with Thanksgiving and continuing through the Christmas season. My Norwegian grandmother started the custom. They are quite a lot of work, but well worth it."

1 cup whipping cream
3 cups flour, approximately
1 cup *unsalted* butter
red-colored sugar for
sprinkling

Pour cream into a small mixing bowl. Add 1 cup flour or a little more. Mix and turn out on a floured pastry canvas. Dough will be soft and sticky. Roll out, adding more flour as necessary, and add little chunks of butter. Double over, roll, add more butter, double over, roll, etc., until all the butter has been used.

"Pick up the dough and throw it on your counter a few times. This sounds silly, but I don't dare *not* do it!"

Chill the dough.

Using a small amount of dough at a time, roll out quite thin using as little flour as possible. Cut into diamond shapes about 2"x3". Sprinkle heavily with red sugar. Bake at 400 degrees F for 7 to 8 minutes, chilling cookie sheet between each baking. Do not overbake, as the tops must not be brown.

Makes about 5 dozen. Store in a large flat box. Do not freeze. Keep in a dry, cool place.

Wedding Spoons

Since the eighteenth century, wedding spoons have been popular at the wedding dinner of the bride in which *rømmegrøt* is the main dish. The bride ate from one spoon and the bridegroom from the other, symbolic of their union. The bride herself was to prepare the pudding, *rømmegrøt*, and a master of ceremonies would talk about the trials and tribulations of making this dish, according to authors Sigrid Marstrander and Erna Oleson Xan in *Time-Honored Norwegian Recipes Adapted to the American Kitchen.*

Left: Wedding spoons from Norway in the Vesterheim collection

Desserts

*This tub of stave construction with double horse-head handle and burnt
decoration is in the Vesterheim collection. Handles in the shape of horse heads
are common in Norwegian folk art. This tub could be used to serve
rømmegrøt.*

*St. Hans Day, the longest day of the year, is celebrated by some festivals
with the serving of rømmegrot. All-night bonfires, singing, dancing, and
merrymaking are held throughout Norway.*

Almond Candy
Marsipan

Sigurd Daasvand of Oslo, Norway

1 lb. sweet almonds, scalded
¹/₄ lb. bitter almonds
1 lb. powdered sugar
1 Tbsp. egg white
food coloring

Grind almonds and bitter almonds finely three or four times. Gradually work into the mixture the powdered sugar and egg white, as necessary.

When dough is smooth and workable, form into tiny loaves of bread, potatoes, fruits, vegetables, or flowers, and color with food coloring. Use cocoa to color potatoes, and prick with toothpick. Strawberries look pretty with artificial leaves added.

Or color several lumps of the dough in different colors, roll them out with rolling pin, brush lightly with egg white, and place one on top of the other. Then cut in small squares or diamonds, and each piece will contain several beautiful colored layers. Candy may also be coated with chocolate.

Please be aware of the danger of eating raw egg.

Fruit Soup or Sweet Soup
Søtsuppe

Gretchen Hansen Quie of St. Paul, Minn., the First Lady of Minnesota, and her husband, Albert, governor of Minnesota, both have Norwegian backgrounds. The governor's family comes from Hallingdal and Mrs. Quie's family from the Stavanger fjord area. Mrs. Quie writes: "Al's Norwegian mother introduced me to søtsuppe or sweet soup and this is my approximation of her recipe. She always had raspberries in her garden and their addition makes it truly 'Nettie's delight'."

1 cup pitted prunes
1 cup raisins
1 cup chopped peeled apple
1 Tbsp. finely chopped orange peel
1 orange, peeled and cut up
4 cups water
1 Tbsp. lemon juice
¹/₄ cup sugar (or more)
1 stick cinnamon
¹/₄ tsp. salt
2 Tbsp. quick-cooking tapioca
1 10-oz. pkg. frozen raspberries

Combine all ingredients except tapioca and raspberries in large saucepan. Simmer for 1 hour.

Sprinkle tapioca over soup and stir to avoid lumping. Cook 15 minutes more. Cool a few minutes. Add frozen raspberries and stir occasionally until they are thawed. Serve hot, or chill and serve with whipped cream. Makes 8 to 10 servings.

Sweet Soup
Søtsuppe

Sonja Strom Scarseth of Aurora, Ill., writes: "My husband Bill and I think it's lucky that our families came from the same area in Norway. It saves so many arguments. We both like Berlinerkranser *instead of* kringle; *we both pour melted better on our lutefisk instead of cream sauce; we both use grape juice in our* søtsuppe. *Our only point of difference: I put sugar on my lefse, and he thinks that is perfectly horrible! 'You wouldn't put sugar on mashed potatoes, would you?' Well, you do have to have something to argue about."*

> **4 cups cranberry-grape juice**
> **1 lemon, thinly sliced**
> **²/₃ cup sugar, approximately**
> **1 stick cinnamon, about 1¹/₂ inches long**
> **1 cup raisins**
> **¹/₄ tsp. salt**
> **2 Tbsp. quick-cooking tapioca**

Combine all ingredients except tapioca in saucepan. Bring to a boil, then cover and simmer 15 to 20 minutes, or until lemon rind is tender and semi-transparent. Add tapioca and boil 2 to 3 minutes, or until tapioca is clear. Soup will still be runny when cool.

Leave the lemon in the soup; it is to be eaten, too. Serve in a sauce dish with Norwegian Christmas cookies. May be served warm, room temperature, or chilled. Serves 8 to 10. Can be frozen 6 to 12 months. Thaw and reheat to recombine ingredients.

Prune Soup
Sviskesuppe

Ruth Christoffer Carlsen of Iowa City, Ia., writes: "My family's story begins in Lærdal, a fishing village at the end of the Sognefjord. My great-grandfather, Kris Kristofferson, did not return from the sea one night and a morning search found him dead in his boat. My great-grandmother, Brita, realized that her five little boys would have no future in Laerdal. What would she live on? So, selling everything possible to finance the trip, she came to Stoughton, Wis., in 1867 with Big Chris, Little Chris, Big Pete, Little Pete, and Lickey.

"The spelling of the name was changed at Ellis Island to Christoffer. Only three of the boys survived: Big Chris, my grandfather, Little Chris, and Lickey.

"Grandfather never forgot a young girl he had known in Lærdal and when he had saved enough money he went back to claim her as his bride and brought her back to Stoughton. Her name was Mari Forthün.

"This is one of her recipes which my mother always served on Good Friday. Though called a soup, it was used as a dessert in our home."

1 pound prunes
4 Tbsp. sago* or tapioca
1 stick cinnamon
1 can pie cherries
1 tsp. lemon juice
sugar

Soak prunes, then boil in water to cover until soft. Remove pits and return prunes to liquid. Add sago and cinnamon stick. Cook until thickened. Add cherries and lemon juice. Sweeten to taste. Serve in bowls with plain cream.

*Sago is a thickening agent used widely in Scandinavia. It must be soaked an hour, and then drained, before using. It is not readily available in the U.S. Tapioca may be substituted.

Fruit Soup
Søtsuppe

Evonne Anderson of Moorhead, Minn.

¹⁄₄ cup sago, soaked in water a few hours
2 cups pitted dried prunes
1 cup dried apricots
1 cup raisins
1 cup dried apple slices
1 stick cinnamon
1 cup grape juice

Combine in a saucepan the sago (after it has been soaked) and its water, dried fruits, cinnamon, and grape juice. Bring to boil, then lower heat and simmer gently until the dried fruits are tender but not falling apart, about 30 minutes. Cool.

If you want it sweeter than the natural sugar in the fruit, add sugar or honey to taste. Can be served warm or cold. Makes 12 servings.

Rhubarb Fruit Soup
Rabarbrasuppe

Barbara Hamre Berg of Decorah, Ia., writes: "I found this recipe in a magazine many years ago. Fruit soups are very Scandinavian."

1 11-oz. can mandarin
    oranges, including syrup
$^1/_2$ cup sugar
3 cups rhubarb, preferably
    red, cut in $^1/_2$-inch pieces

Drain oranges, reserving syrup. In a one-quart saucepan, combine reserved syrup, sugar, and rhubarb. Bring to a boil, cover, and cook over low heat until rhubarb is tender, but still retains its shape, about 5 minutes. Remove from heat; stir in mandarin oranges. Chill. Spoon into sherbet dishes. Serve with whipped cream, if desired. Serves four.

"I prefer no cream. I make it one batch at a time. It freezes very well and we like it with ice crystals still in it."

Hagletta

Erma W. Fruland of Newark, Ill., is the great-great-granddaughter of Daniel Stenson Rosdail, who was part owner of the sloop Restauration, *which brought the first Norwegian emigrants to this country in 1825.*

    2 quarts milk
    5 eggs, beaten
    1 cup sugar
    salt
    4 cups buttermilk

Bring milk to a slow boil. Mix well-beaten eggs, sugar, salt, and buttermilk. Add all at once to boiling milk. Do not stir until mixture has formed curds on top. Break, then fold over gently with a large spatula. Let boil slowly for about 40 minutes. Chill. Serve when ice cold.

Barbara Hamre Berg of Decorah, Ia., contributed her version of *Hagletta* and said: "It is traditionally served at the end of a meal, but I like a large bowl of it for breakfast! I believe it is a recipe from the coastal areas of Norway because it has no counterpart in the Valdres area of Norway from where my ancestors came."

Norwegian Fruit Soup
Søtsuppe

Marilyn Skaugstad of Iowa City, Ia.

    1 cup pitted prunes
    1 cup white or dark seedless
        raisins or a mixture
    $^1/_2$ cup currants
    2 cups chopped rhubarb
    3 cups water
    1 cup sugar
    $^1/_2$ cup quick-cooking tapioca
    1 stick cinnamon
    $^1/_4$ tsp. salt
    2 cups grape juice (or part
        grape wine)
    juice of 1 lemon

Combine all ingredients except grape juice and lemon juice. Bring to a slow boil. Turn down heat, cover, and simmer until tapioca is clear. Stir frequently to keep tapioca from sticking to bottom of pan. Add grape juice and lemon juice and again bring to a boil. Serve hot or cold.

"It can be served with milk or cream for breakfast. It makes 10 to 12 small servings."

Interior of the Norwegian home, Old World Wisconsin, at Eagle

Lemon Custard in Cups
Citron pudding i kopper

Linda Wangsness Triebes, Des Moines, Iowa, writes: "I am a full-blooded Norwegian, married to David Triebes, with a two-year-old son, Erik. I stay home to care for my son and work on my art, Norwegian rosemaling, gnome art, and children's art. Most of my activities center on my strong Norwegian background, from traveling to Norway to continuing to meet Norwegian friends to keeping my family's heritage alive.

"This recipe came from my grandmother, Christina Lotvedt Anderson of Decorah, Iowa, my hometown. She was a boarding house cook, school cook, and restaurant owner, which gave her the reputation as the best cook around."

    2 Tbsp. butter
    1 cup sugar
    3 eggs, separated
    4 Tbsp. flour
    1/4 tsp. salt
    5 Tbsp. lemon juice
    rind of 1 lemon
    1 1/2 cups milk

Cream butter, sugar, and egg yolks and beat thoroughly. Add flour, salt, lemon juice, and rind. Add milk. Fold in stiffly beaten egg whites. Pour into greased custard cups. Set cups in pan of water, approximately $1/4$- to $1/2$-inch deep, and bake 45 minutes at 350 degrees F. When done, each cup will contain custard at the bottom and sponge cake on top. Makes 8 servings.

Country and City Rømmegrøt

Hilda Nelson of Fergus Falls, Minn., mother of Marion Nelson, director of the Norwegian-American Museum in Decorah, Ia., sent recipes for two versions of the popular dish Rømmegrøt. *Hilda spent her childhood in Norway. She says, "No measurements were used for the many kinds of* grøt. *True country* rømmegrøt *was made with very thick sour cream. City* rømmegrøt *was made like drawn butter gravy, except thicker. It was made from butter instead of cream. Modern Norwegian Americans prefer sweet rather than sour cream."*

Country Rømmegrøt

- **3 cups sour cream**
- **2 cups flour**
- **2$1/4$ quarts boiling milk**
- **1 tsp. salt**

Boil cream $1/2$ hour; sift in flour gradually, stirring constantly. As the butterfat comes out, take off with a spoon and add rest of flour. Thin with boiling milk. Boil, remove from heat and add salt.

City Rømmegrøt

- **$1/2$ cup butter or margarine**
- **1 cup flour**
- **1 quart milk, scalded**
- **1 tsp. salt**
- **5 Tbsp. sugar**
- **cinnamon**

Melt butter or margarine in a heavy pan. Add 1 cup flour slowly as when making cream sauce. Watch carefully so that it doesn't scorch. Add scalded milk a little at a time. Mix and beat until smooth and thick. Add salt and sugar. Mix and pour into serving dish. Sprinkle sugar and cinnamon on top. Serve with melted butter on the side.

Evonne Anderson of Moorhead, Minn., wrote: "The pioneers used this as a main dish; today's Norwegians have a small dish for dessert. It can be made with milk if you don't want it so rich. My husband's grandfather homesteaded in North Dakota, and he said they even made it with water when they didn't have milk . . ."

Cream Pudding
Fløtegrøt

Thora Leonard of Story City, Ia., whose parents were born in Norway, says: "I grew up in an American home with beautiful Norwegian accents, as well as truly loyal American ideals!

"This pudding was called sende mat *in the Norwegian community in which I lived as a child. It was customary for ladies to prepare this delicacy to take to a new mother in the neighborhood. Mothers then were confined to bed for longer periods of time after a baby was born, and babies were born at home, so women were frequently seen carrying a bowl of* sende mat *into a friend's house."*

> 4 cups sweet cream
> 1 cup flour
> 2 cups warm milk
> $^1/_2$ tsp. salt
> sugar, cinnamon, raisins as
>   topping

Bring cream to a boil. Let boil for 10 minutes. Simmer slowly while sifting flour into cream. Stir constantly until smooth and thick. When butterfat appears, remove it and save to use as a topping. Add warm milk, stirring to prevent scorching. Keep beating until mixture appears smooth and velvety. Add salt and continue stirring for about a minute.

"Pour into your prettiest china bowl and serve hot, topped with the butterfat which you dipped from the pudding as it was boiling. Add sugar, cinnamon, and/or raisins, making a delicious and attractive topping for this special Norwegian dessert. It makes about six generous servings."

Kiss Pudding

Ethel Kvalheim of Stoughton, Wis., sent this recipe. A well-known rosemaler, she was one of the earliest winners of the Medal of Honor for work in rosemaling.

> 4 eggs, separated
> $^1/_4$ cup sugar
> dash of salt
> 2 cups milk, scalded
> 1 tsp. vanilla
> $^2/_3$ cup powdered sugar
> 2 squares chocolate, melted

Beat egg yolks slightly. Add sugar, salt, and slightly cooled milk. Cook in double boiler, stirring constantly until mixture coats spoon. Add vanilla. Spoon into serving dishes.

Beat egg whites until stiff. Fold in powdered sugar and melted chocolate. Put on top of custard. Chill and serve. Serves 4.

Old-Fashioned Custard Pudding with Oranges
Gammeldags krempudding med appelsiner

John K. Hanson, founder of Winnebago Industries, Inc., in Forest City, Ia.

- **4 cups milk**
- **3 eggs, lightly beaten**
- **2 Tbsp. cornstarch**
- **³/₄ cup sugar**
- **1 tsp. vanilla**
- **2 to 3 oranges, peeled and diced**

Scald milk in top of double boiler. In a mixing bowl, beat eggs. In a small bowl, mix cornstarch and sugar. Add to beaten eggs. Pour scalded milk over eggs, cornstarch and sugar, stirring constantly. Return to top of double boiler and cook until custard adheres to spoon and is smooth.

Add vanilla. Put orange pieces in large serving bowl. Pour pudding over, mix gently, and allow to cool.

"This is a delicious and nourishing family favorite. Mom served it family style in the traditional Bavarian china bowl with fruit painted on the base (one of her wedding presents) as a noon-time dessert."

Rice Pudding
Risengrynsgrøt

Inez G. Schaefer of Rochester, Minnesota, is a member of the board of directors of the Norwegian-American Museum.

- **1 cup water**
- **¹/₂ cup long-grained rice**
- **¹/₂ tsp. salt**
- **4 cups milk**
- **¹/₄ cup butter**
- **2 eggs**
- **¹/₂ cup sugar**
- **1 tsp. vanilla**
- **¹/₂ cup raisins**
- **nutmeg**

Bring water, rice and salt to a boil and cook 7 minutes. Add milk and butter; bring to a boil. Reduce heat, cover, and simmer for 1 to 1¹/₄ hours. Beat eggs, sugar, and vanilla and add to rice mixture. Remove from heat and add raisins.

Turn into 13"x9" pan and sprinkle with nutmeg. Cover with plastic wrap and chill. May also be served warm.

Nutty Pumpkin Pie

Vi Thode of Stoughton, Wis., is a nationally noted rosemaler who won the gold medal from the National Rosemaling Exhibit at the Norwegian-American Museum in 1970. She has written four books on rosemaling and has taught rosemaling 20 years.

Although pumpkin pie is uniquely American and certainly not an original Norwegian recipe, it is a favorite to serve Norwegians visiting in American homes. In Decorah, one family serves pie to visiting rosemaling teachers because pie is a dessert unfamiliar to Norwegians.

Marion Nelson, director of Vesterheim, said that in Norway pumpkins are fed to the animals so Norwegians visiting America who are served pumpkin pie "approach it very cautiously and end up loving it."

> 1 16-oz. can pumpkin
> 5 eggs
> 1¹/₂ cups sugar
> 1 tsp. salt
> 2 heaping Tbsp. flour
> 2 tsp. cinnamon
> 2 tsp. nutmeg
> 2 tsp. mace
> 1 tsp. allspice
> 1 tsp. ginger
> ¹/₂ tsp. cloves
> 2 tsp. vanilla
> 3¹/₂ cups milk
> 2 uncooked pie crusts
> ¹/₂ cup finely chopped walnuts, hickory nuts, or pecans
> prepared whipped cream

Put pumpkin in electric mixer bowl, add eggs and mix well. In a two-cup measuring cup, put sugar, salt, flour and spices. Mix and add to mixer bowl. Let mix. Add vanilla and milk and mix until well-blended. Pour into two uncooked pie crusts. Sprinkle half of nuts on each pie. Set pies on one large cookie sheet or two small ones. Bake 1 hour at 375 degrees F or until done.

This pie freezes well. Serve with dollops of whipped cream. Two pies will serve 10 people.

Lemon Fromage with Raspberry Sauce
Sitronfromasj med bringebærsaus

Estelle Knudsen of Eden Prairie, Minn., is the founder of the Nordic Brunch and Nordic Dinner. Estelle writes: "The dinner was designed for the overflow from the sold-out brunch. It is a joint venture of Norwegian-American Museum members from St. Paul and

Minneapolis. This recipe, for the 1980 Nordic Dinner, came from Norway."

1 3-oz. pkg. lemon-flavored gelatin
1 cup hot water
1 cup orange juice, strained
1 cup heavy cream, whipped
1¹/₂ tsp. grated lemon rind
Sauce:
1 10-oz. pkg. frozen raspberries
³/₄ cup red currant jelly
1 Tbsp. cornstarch
sugar

Dissolve gelatin in hot water. Add orange juice and refrigerate until the consistency of egg whites. Remove from refrigerator and beat until frothy. Fold in whipped cream and lemon rind. Pour into chilled and lightly oiled mold. Chill. When firm, unmold. Serve with fresh raspberries and raspberry sauce.

To make sauce, press thawed raspberries through food mill. Heat together ³/₄ cup of this purée with the currant jelly. Blend cornstarch into remaining ¹/₄ cup of the purée. Add to jelly mixture and cook until thick and clear. Sprinkle with granulated sugar to prevent a layer from forming on top. Cool. Makes 8 servings.

Curds and Whey
Dravle

Norma Anderson Wangsness of Decorah, Iowa. "This is a recipe made by my mother Christine Lotvedt Anderson. The way Mother turned the cheese chunks with such tender care was truly an art form. My big brother liked the curds and I loved the whey so there were no family feuds over dravle."

2 quarts sweet milk
2 eggs
1 quart buttermilk
1¹/₂ cups sugar
1 cup raisins
3 Tbsp. cornstarch
3 Tbsp. cream or milk

Cook sweet milk until it comes to a boil. Beat eggs into buttermilk and add to hot milk slowly. When cheese settles, turn down heat for 15 to 20 minutes and simmer. Then turn heat up and cook ¹/₂ hour or more. Add the sugar and raisins. Thicken with the cornstarch mixed with cream or milk. When finished, you have curds and whey. When cooking, handle very gently so as not to break the cheese curds. A wooden spoon is good to stir with. You may turn cheese chunks *gently* several times while cooking.

Black and White Fluff
Sitronfromage med frukt

Gina J. Hanson Hanson, Forest City, Iowa, the mother of John K. Hanson and Barbara Hanson Bulman.

"A family favorite all through the years when the children were at home. It's easily and quickly put together and can be made ahead and ready to serve for any special meal. Serving in your footed crystal makes it attractive."

1¹/₂ cups prunes
2 bananas
12 marshmallows
2 cups whipping cream
¹/₂ tsp. lemon extract
maraschino cherries

Wash prunes and boil in enough water to cover until tender, about 10 minutes. Drain and chill. Remove pits, and cut prunes into small pieces. Slice bananas; dip in lemon juice to prevent discoloring. Cut marshmallows into eight pieces each. Whip cream. Add lemon extract, prunes, bananas and marshmallows. Mix lightly. Serve in footed glass dishes. Top each serving with a maraschino cherry.

Variation: You can use miniature marshmallows and whipped topping to simplify the preparation of this dessert.

"Veiled Peasant Girls"
Tilslørte bondepiker

Sigurd Daasvand was editor of the Norwegian newspaper Nordisk Tidende *in Brooklyn, N.Y., for 11 years before retiring in 1982 to Oslo, Norway.*

2 cups dark bread crumbs or
graham cracker crumbs
2 Tbsp. butter
applesauce or raspberry jam
whipped cream

Grate stale, dark bread or graham cracker crumbs; brown in frying pan in butter. If bread crumbs are used, add a tablespoon of sugar. When mixture is cool, place in a pudding dish in layers alternately with flavored applesauce or raspberry jam. Refrigerate overnight, or a few hours, and serve with whipped cream.

Sour Milk and Flatbread
Hedmark flatbrødsoll

Rolf H. Erickson of Evanston, Ill., is on the board of directors of Vesterheim and the Norwegian-American Historical Association. He documents histories of immigrants by collecting their artifacts and archival material.

"When cousin Jenny Knutsen

served us dinner at her apartment in Hamar, Norway, the summer of 1979 she served a dessert called flatbrødsoll.

"She cautioned, 'You might not like this, but it is a dish great-grandfather Knut Ramseth would surely have known. It's an old Hedmark specialty.' It was soured milk spooned over crumbled flatbread. I liked it very much and have made something like it."

> 1 16-oz. carton low-calorie plain yogurt
> 2 cups low-fat dry cottage cheese
> 2 percent lowfat milk
> Ideal flatbread
> sugar (optional)

Mix yogurt, cottage cheese and enough milk to make mixture the consistency of a sauce.

"I bring it to the table cold in a sauce dish and let my guests serve themselves by spooning it over crumbled Ideal flatbread. Sugar may be sprinkled over the top. This makes a refreshing first course with *smørbrød,* ideal for summer and ideal for those of us who watch calories."

Nordic Crêpes
Norsk pannekaker

Janice Loomis of Rockford, Michigan, is a folk art teacher and an award winner in rosemaling and folk art.

> 1¼ cups flour
> 2 Tbsp. sugar
> pinch salt
> 3 eggs
> 1½ cups milk
> 2 Tbsp. butter, melted
> ½ tsp. lemon, rum, or brandy extract

Filling:
> butter
> strawberry jam
> powdered sugar
> fresh strawberries

Place all ingredients in blender or mixer and beat well. Let batter stand for 1 hour for more perfect crêpes. Use crêpe pan according to directions.

Spread each crêpe with softened butter and strawberry jam. Roll and sprinkle with powdered sugar. Serve with fresh or frozen strawberries.

Norwegian Waffles
Hjemlengsel

Josefa Hansen Andersen of Chicago tells us these waffles are served at many Norwegian Seamen's churches throughout the world. The Norwegian name for the waffles means "longing for home." Mrs. Andersen is treasurer of the Viking Ship Restoration Committee. Her husband Harry is a member of the board of directors of Vesterheim, the Norwegian-American Museum in Decorah, Iowa.

> **2 eggs**
> $1/4$ **cup sugar**
> $1^1/2$ **cups flour**
> $1^1/2$ **tsp. baking powder**
> **1 tsp. baking soda**
> $1/2$ **tsp. salt**
> $1/4$ **tsp. ground cardamom**
> **2 cups buttermilk**
> **2 Tbsp. melted butter**

Beat eggs and sugar until light and creamy. Mix all dry ingredients and add them to the sugar mixture alternately with the buttermilk. Add melted butter. Brown waffles in waffle iron. These waffles are soft in texture. Serve cold with butter, lingonberries or fruit preserves. They are also served with *gjetost* (goat cheese). Makes 8 to 10 waffles.

Norwegian Pancakes
Pannekaker

Ruth Christoffer Carlsen of Iowa City, Ia., is the author of eight books for young people, published by Houghton-Mifflin Publishing Company. She writes: "This recipe we use all the time. The pancakes are much like crêpes, but we use them for breakfast with cinnamon and sugar and then roll them. In Norway we found they filled them with lingonberries or strawberries plus whipped cream, and we are enthusiastic about that filling."

> **3 eggs**
> **1 cup flour**
> $1^1/2$ **cups milk**
> $1/8$ **tsp. salt**
> **dash cinnamon**

Beat eggs slightly with fork. Stir in flour. Add milk and other ingredients and stir until smooth. Batter should be thin. Use a 7-inch skillet with sloped sides. Heat skillet. Pour in small amount of oil. Dip $1/4$ cup batter, pour in hot pan and quickly tip pan to spread batter over bottom. Slip spatula under cake when top side looks dry. Flip over and brown on other side. Takes only a few seconds. Fold in half or roll on plate.

"To fill, open pancake flat on

plate and place a line of butter straight across its center. Cover butter with jam or a sprinkling of sugar and cinnamon (my favorite filling as a child).

"Today we prefer sour cream over raspberries, strawberries or lingonberries with a dusting of powdered sugar. Roll pancake to eat."

Grandmother's Buttermilk Doughnuts

Agnes Kjome of Decorah, who is a volunteer at Vesterheim

**1 egg, well-beaten
1¹/₂ cups fresh thick buttermilk
4 cups flour
1 tsp. soda
1 tsp. salt
¹/₂ tsp. cinnamon
¹/₄ tsp. nutmeg
1 cup sugar
4 Tbsp. melted vegetable shortening
1 tsp. vanilla (optional)
oil for frying**

Mix beaten egg and milk. Put flour, soda, salt, spices and sugar in large bowl. Add egg and milk mixture. Add melted shortening and mix well. Add vanilla, if desired. Turn out on lightly floured board.

Roll dough out to 1/3-inch thickness. Cut and fry in hot oil at 425 degrees F, turning when doughnuts rise to top. Doughnuts should be a golden brown on both sides and puffed out.

Keep oil at same temperature throughout frying. Don't try to fry too many doughnuts at one time. Allow space for floating.

Remove carefully to a paper-covered cookie sheet to drain.

Doughnuts may be dipped or rolled in sugar, powdered sugar or icing. Makes 2 to 2¹/₂ dozen doughnuts 2¹/₂-inches in diameter. Can be frozen or kept in cool place to retain freshness.

Miniature viking ship of enamel in a filigree frame, contributed to Vesterheim by Estelle Knudsen and her sister Margaret Smaby, in memory of their mother, Amelia Holm-Hagen. Vesterheim photo

Christmas Baking

by Marilyn Skaugstad

All the recipes are family favorites from my mother and her mother, Torbjorg. A snack we had at Grandma's was called *skjebrod*, a slice of homemade bread served with milk. Who would have thought, as I sat with my elbows propped on Grandma Olson's big kitchen table watching her bake, that sixty years later I would be recalling her Norwegian heritage and customs and foods . . . With flour and dough flying, she told me about her summers as a little girl spent high in the mountains above the Sørfjorden Fjord making flatbread on an old wood-fired cookstove in a little cabin while she tended the sheep for her family.

With her "letter" in hand, she came to America in the early 1900s and worked for a family in Wisconsin. Eventually she married my grandfather, Ole J. Olson, whose family also came from Norway. They farmed a beautiful big farm in Humboldt County, Iowa.

My father, L.E. Mosbach, of Irish-German descent, used to tease my mother, Esther, saying that Norwegian girls made the best wives, one of the reasons being that they were wonderful cooks.

We have all visited Grandma Olson's farm in Ullensvang, Norway, where our relatives still live. When I married my husband, Charles, I certainly reinforced my Norwegian heritage. His father came from Land, Norway, to Bode, Iowa, where he met and married Albie Tufte, whose family came from Telemark. Bode, a very Norwegian community, still has annual smorgasbord suppers. My four sisters-in-law and I enjoy sharing recipes and customs from Norway. Christmas is always full of good food from Norwegian family recipes—lutefisk, lefse, meatballs.

Back cover:

Marilyn Skaugstad baked the goodies shown. Clockwise from the top, the foods include haring kake *and* spiced hermits. *The tray holds* rosettes, spritz, kringle, *potato cakes,* sandbakkels, *and* krumkake. Julekake *is the Norwegian Tea Ring. Fruit soup is in the compote. The antique rosemaled wooden bowl contains nuts. The tablecloth with Hardanger embroidery was made by Marilyn's grandmother Torbjorg Gunnerson-Sekse Olson, who brought it to America in the early 1900s. The silver spoons are from her family in Norway.*

This still life at Vesterheim represents a traditional Christmas Eve meal of decorated butter, flatbread on a wood-turned pedestal, and fish pudding molded in the form of a fish. A devotional book contains daily scriptural readings, basic to the family library.

Norwegian Table Prayer

I Jesu navn går vi til bords,
Å spise og drikke på dit ord.
Deg Gud til ære, oss til gavn,
Så får vi mat i Jesu navn.
Amen

Darrell Henning, Vesterheim photo
Heddal Stave Church